Loss—An

Dedication

To my dear friend Lis
who pushed me out of a cosy nest,
sure that I could fly.

Other books and publications by Jean C. Grigor

Grow to Love (Saint Andrew Press, 1980)

A Tool for Christians ⎫ Department of Education
A Tool for Christians, book two ⎭ of the Church of Scotland, 1983

Growing Fellowship (Woman's Guild of the Church of Scotland 1982)

What on earth is God like? (Wild Goose Publications, 1985)

Building Relationships ⎫
Challenging Relationships ⎪ Four out of a series published
Family Relationships ⎬ by the Bible Society in 1985
Work Relationships ⎭

The last six of these publications are Bible study books for groups

The quotations from the *Good News Bible* are by permission of the publishers

The Grief Process by Yorick Spiegel is published by the SCM Press

The poem *My Father is Dying* is in a collection of Alastair Reid's work called *Weathering* published by The Canongate Press

Where sources have not been able to be traced, acknowledgement will be made in future editions of this book if these are made known to the publisher

Loss—An invitation to grow

by

Jean C. Grigor

Published by Arthur James
One Cranbourne Road,
London, N10 2BT

First published in 1986
© Jean C. Grigor 1986

Published in 1986 by Arthur James Ltd.,
One Cranbourne Road, London N10 2BT, England

British Library Cataloguing in Publication Data

Grigor, Jean C.

Loss—An invitation to grow.
1. Bereavement—Psychological aspects
2. Deprivation (Psychology)
I. Title
306.8'8   BF575.G7

ISBN 0-85305-269-7

Printed in Great Britain by
Richard Clay (The Chaucer Press) Ltd.,
Bungay, Suffolk

The light shines in the darkness, and the darkness has never put it out.

John 1 : 5 (Good News Bible)

ACKNOWLEDGMENTS

I have written this book because God has given me so much through other people and in life's experiences.

Jesus constantly used stories in his teaching. I love to do the same. I want to thank all the many people who have given me permission to write parts of their stories in this book but under names different from their own.

Over the years, those I have taught have been generous with their feedback to me on the effectiveness of both the content and the method I have used with them. Because of that, the content of this book is other than it might have been.

Jean Steele laboured so patiently over a number of years with parts of this manuscript. I am very much indebted to her.

Many friends have read all or parts of the manuscript and have given me insightful and useful suggestions for its improvement. In particular I thank Sandie, my aunt Elsie Wood, the McLeans, the Moodies, the Lawsons, the Loughs, the Patersons, the Weirs, and Jenny.

My husband, Bill, is one of my best manuscript critics, but I want to thank him most of all, along with our children, Julie and Jim, for allowing and indeed encouraging me to work with and for other people in time they might have claimed was theirs.

GROW THROUGH LOSS

To survive birth

        is to pass through
        the experience of loss common to all
           humanity
        with an invitation to live

To grow through   that loss
        requires the will to live
               the support of others
               the forgetting of the pain
      in the need to adapt to life without the
        womb

To ask more loss

        seems strange—
      yet, time and again we risk grief
      by giving ourselves to a place
                 to a job
                 to a possession
                 to a dream
                 to an ability
                 to mortal and fallible
                    beings

to find at their loss

      an invitation to pain—
      another invitation to grow

Loss—An invitation to grow

CHAPTER ONE

How I came to grief

Some memories are hard to forget.

She was in the Infirmary, dying of a brain tumour. I was not looking forward to visiting her again, and had decided to leave it till tomorrow, or the next day, or ... it was only Wednesday. Driving home from town I had to pass the hospital. An inner voice urged 'Go and see her *now*, Jean'.

That was in the days when dying and grieving people brought me face to face with fears with which I had not yet learned to cope. I was a parish deaconess, not long out of college.

I parked my car and went in. The staff nurse said 'She's unconscious, her parents are with her'. I would have loved to have said 'I'll not trouble them. I'll just go' but the deaconess in me pushed me towards the screened bed, my legs trembling beneath the skirt of my grey uniform.

The elderly parents were sitting by the bedside, helplessly, not looking at the form lying still under the white sheet. As I parted the screens they looked up and acknowledged me with their dazed, exhausted eyes.

I could think of nothing to say to them! Inside, I panicked. I wanted to run away, but I couldn't. 'Only a few minutes' the nurse had said. How could I make these pass so that I could go?

'Would you like me to read the twenty-third psalm?' I heard myself saying. The old man nodded, and sniffed. He was very close to tears.

I reached out to hold the hand of the unconscious girl. Her father reached out to hold her other hand. I read the familiar

words to help my own panic and embarrassment. I cannot now
remember whether or not I prayed aloud with the parents, but
I shook their hands, and left. I had no more words. Nor had
they.

My walk back to my car was through a fog of failure. How I
wished I had not gone there. Why did I not know what to do?
Why could I not think of anything to say to them? All I had
done was add embarrassment to their pain. I should have left
them alone. The minister should have gone instead. How could
I presume to represent Christ to those who mourned when
that experience had not yet met me personally?

When I heard later that the girl had died that same afternoon, I felt even more inadequate for my pastoral task.

A week later, I was passing through the church hall when,
to my consternation (for once again I thought 'I don't know
what to say!'), I saw the elderly bereaved father detach himself
from a group and walk towards me. He reached out his hand
to take mine. There were tears in his eyes. 'You would hear?',
he said. I nodded. 'I just want to say thank you for coming
that day. You brought strength.'

I took myself to the vestry and sat down. Again I felt so
weak . . . Could I really have brought strength?

A Widow

Another incident is etched vividly upon my mind. I had
gone to visit a widow in her fifties around three o'clock on
a winter's afternoon. It did not take long for her to begin
to pour out to me all she had been bottling up for
months.

I became aware that she was talking on, expecting no reply
from me. She seemed almost to be giving some sort of un-
selfconscious performance. I sat in an armchair, hardly able to
take my eyes off her, feeling quite unable to terminate my
visit and go on to another home on my visiting list. The

afternoon wore on, and the darkness began to fall. She made no attempt to put on a light. As we sat there in the gathering dark, she told me story after story of her dead husband coming back to visit her. I remember her saying that when she went into church, he would slip into the pew beside her.

At first I was transfixed by the weird way she told me of her experiences, but as the darkness deepened I became scared. I sat there, wondering whether or not I was shut up alone in a house with a mad woman. At the same time, I felt a childish fear that, if I stood up to go, her husband's ghost might grab me round the ankles!

I had never read of such experiences and no one had taught me to expect common grief reactions like this during my pastoral visitation.

What I did or said to end that visit, I no longer remember, but I am sure that my actions would stem from my fright and my need to get back safely into the street again. I was too upset to be in touch with any loving compassion that I felt for the widow who had chosen to share with me something so precious and intimate in the continuing relationship she so much wanted with her deceased husband.

An Opportunity

During the years I served as parish deaconess I must have visited hundreds of dying or grieving people, yet that was the part of my ministry which continued to distress me. So often I left with feelings of helplessness.

After some years in parish work, I was given the opportunity of a scholarship year in the USA. I eagerly took the classes offered in pastoral psychology, in counselling the dying, and one particularly where I had the opportunity to work on a special project on widowhood.

Somehow, I felt that, during the years of working with the dying and bereaved, I had picked up a recognition of all the individual letters of an alphabet. At last I was being taught how to read and write! The letters which at times had seemed so strange and unrelated to each other, now fell into place and I could make sense of them. The process of grieving was a very painful one for many people, but it was a normal, healing process designed by the Spirit of God. Since he had given us the potential for loving, he had, with that gift, to make provision for the growth of new life and meaning at the loss of a loved one. 'Happy are those who mourn' claimed his Son. 'God will comfort them.'

By the end of that year in which so much had been so helpful to me, I knew I would no longer have to minister to those in grief, while feeling dominated by my helpless fears. It was a huge relief! Yet, knowing how black the experience could be for others, I was still afraid of having, one day, to face the pain of personal bereavement for myself.

Two years after my return to the parish, a friend offered me a position in Australia. In many ways I felt attracted to it, but it was such a long way from home, and my parents had both entered their seventies. While I was considering this offer, I had a dream. In it, my mother and I seemed to be walking round the inside rim of an enormous well. She slipped and fell down inside, and there was no way I could catch her. In the light of the next day I knew my nightmare had sprung from my fear of her dying, yet she enjoyed excellent health. With her full approval and blessing, I decided to go to work in Australia.

Almost three years later, when I was within a month or two of returning home to work in Scotland, she had a heart attack and died the following day. It was impossible to reach her before she died. My nightmare had become a reality and I had begun to experience, for myself, a time of very painful grief.

I was able to fly home for her funeral, but it was not until two and a half years later, at a House Church training week, that the leader whom I greatly loved and respected, helped me to 'say goodbye' to my mother, and come to terms with my loss.

More than a decade has passed since my mother's death. These years have meant for me further experiences of loss and personal grief, a great deal of training, learning and reading, many more privileged experiences of being with others while they have worked through their grief . . . and a desire to pass on what I have learned to other people.

A Universal Experience

Loss is a universal experience. No-one can escape it in some form. Grieving follows loss and each individual grieves uniquely.

Some remain very much alone in their grief and choose to use the energy they once used for the lost relationship to maintain it in fantasy. Others grow through their grief, gradually withdrawing the energy from the mourned relationship as they re-invest it in new ones.

Grieving can be this growing process. There are many who go through it, apparently by themselves, and do it well. But most benefit in their grief from the loving support of others. They will need help when they tumble somewhere along the way to becoming whole again.

Through grieving, I have grown to value the visible church and to be aware of the invisible church. Grieving has given me a new relationship with the risen Christ and that affects my *human* relationships.

Hope

I am glad that the Spirit gives life and love and hope. I am very glad that the Spirit of God sweeps, like the wind, throughout the world, utterly beyond the limitations of humankind.

This book cannot say all there is to say about being with grieving people, but in it there may be insights and guidelines to help us see what human beings can do for each other while the Spirit works on within us.

CHAPTER TWO

Any logs in your eye?

First take the log out of your own eye, and then you will be able to see clearly to take the speck out of your brother's eye.

Matthew 7:5 (GNB)

A common technique in television comedy is to let the viewer into the secret fantasies of the hero as he imagines how wonderfully he will act in a given situation, only to follow it up with the reality of all the gaffes he makes when the event itself takes place. Personal fantasies can be so out of touch with reality that they can be like the log Jesus mentioned, blocking out our ability to see how to handle life as it is.

In my opening chapter I shared two memories of incidents where I felt I had failed badly in my ministry to grieving people.

I had not known what to say to the parents of the dying girl. I had had in my mind a super-image of an ideal comforter—of someone who knew instinctively the wisest possible words that would bring instant comfort and inspiration—words which would, of course, be enshrined for ever in the memories of the grieving parents.

My fantasy was that the parents ought to have been able to say something like this after my visit: 'You can imagine how we felt there in the hospital, with our daughter at death's very door. But just when despair was about to engulf us completely, we looked up . . . and there was the deaconess! I'll never forget what she said to us then. Her very words were . . .' (at this

point in my fantasy words failed me again!) '. . . and from that
moment on, we knew we could face the dark days ahead with a
faith that would pierce the shadows and triumph over every
weakness.'

What an ego-trip! My disillusionment and distress came
from not living up to a soap opera fantasy. It had nothing
whatsoever to do with the kind of ministry God had in mind
for me. I had a log in my eye!

Looking back now, with that log mercifully removed, I can
see how the Holy Spirit, in spite of my muddled ideas, guided
me that day to be able to bring *his* strength into *their* weakness.
I had felt him asking me to go to that Infirmary. I had to
go. People can feel greatly cut off and alone in times of great
suffering. The fact that even a fearful and inexperienced
young deaconess arrived at that point would remind them that
they belonged to the wider Christian community, that others
cared.

I had instinctively reached out to take the girl's hand and
her father had done the same. Before I left, I had shaken
hands with the girl's parents, not knowing what to say. Now I
know that for a human being in distress, a warm touch can
penetrate through the numbness of grief to places words
cannot reach. The only words which came to me to use were
the words of the twenty-third psalm—'The Lord is my Shep-
herd . . .' For centuries God's people have been reassured and
comforted by these words. Somehow, their very familiarity is
soothing. After I left, the parents would still have these words
echoing in their minds, reminding them of God's presence in
their journey through the dark valley.

In makes sense to me now that the elderly father told me
later that I had brought strength. If I had fulfilled my fantasy,
he would have had to come and tell me how wise I was, and
how I could have polished my halo with my illusions of
grandeur! But the story of my visit to the widow was a sad
failure in ministry.

I had sat in the woman's home for about two hours, inwardly

rejecting her by thinking her 'weird' and 'mad', and privately condeming her for dabbling with departed spirits. I can well understand the fears that had predisposed some to burn witches in the past! I had wanted rid of that woman and what she was telling me. Somehow I felt that she might be tainting me if I stayed, yet that some evil power from her was keeping me in the room. All these things became a huge 'log' in my eye, blinding me to her needs. There I was, the representative of the loving Christian community in her parish, sent by them to love and support her, and instead I was blaming her for my fear and helplessness! I wanted to escape from a lonely woman who was trusting me enough to tell me how greatly she longed that her husband could be alive and well and with her again.

The only thing wrong with that widow in her grief was that she did not fit my image of what widows should say to those who visit them! It would have been totally acceptable to me if she had cried a little, dried her tears, then said quietly 'I'm so sorry, Miss Grigor. I know I should be glad that he is at rest. It's just that I miss him so much.' To which I would have replied magnaminously, 'I quite understand, Mrs Brown. Please don't apologise for breaking down. I know you'll try to be brave in future. Life must go on.' In my mind, widows were expected to shed a few tears, then to put up a brave front while they coped with their own private readjustment to living without their husbands. They were expected neither to burden others, nor to scare them!

If I then sum up my attitudes to the bereaved at the beginning of my ministry, they would be something like these:

1. I would be doing well as a comforter if I said the right words.
2. The bereaved were acceptable to me if they cried, but they then had to regain control, so that they would not upset others—especially me.

Perhaps you are smiling at my naïveté. You may, on the

other hand, be feeling quite alarmed at the damage I might have done working among vulnerable people with such prejudiced, unexamined attitudes. I wish now that someone had given me some help to become aware of the logs in my eye, so that I could have seen myself more clearly and only then looked at others with the compassion they deserved.

I can safely assume that if you are reading this book you are someone who cares about others, especially those who are grieving. If you have always found your time with them easy and straightforward, giving you no pain or problem, you will not be interested in what this book has to offer. If, on the other hand, you are aware that you have not always coped perfectly in this ministry, I invite you to look at these attitudes—and perhaps the prejudices you may be carrying with you as you go to comfort those who mourns.

Attitude Formation

The formation of attitudes begins at a very early stage in a person's life. No matter how skilfully adults imagine they are shielding a young child from painful exposure to grief or grieving people, that child will have his or her highly perceptive radar switched on, alert for all kinds of signals of distress. Because a young child has little experience of life, there is often a breakdown in the effectiveness of his or her interpretation of the signals received. Those early feelings, and perhaps false conclusions, are registered in the child's awareness and may be dormant only to be reactivated many years later by a signal similar to the one received in early childhood.

As far as I can recall, my first experience of mourning came when I was two years old. I have since been given the information that my grandmother died then, and that she died, not only in my home, but in my bed. I have no conscious memories of the old lady, but I know that my mother had to nurse her mother-in-law until she died and I know that she did not like her very much.

rely now think of my father's mother, but if I do, I get unny frightened feeling, though I have no idea why. It must have been something I picked up at the time—perhaps something I noticed in my mother's attitude. And that same, odd little feeling comes to me momentarily even yet if I hear that someone has died peacefully in bed! It does not upset me, but it comes, in spite of the fact that I know that for most people it would be desirable to die at home in bed with family around. Feelings and attitudes are not always 'reasonable'. Very often, if they spring from early experiences, it is impossible to trace their origins.

My second exposure to bereavement was when I was around six or seven, during the second world war. The father of the family next door was a sea captain. His ship was torpedoed, and he was killed. I have memories of his widow crying and of my mother crying with her when the news came through. As far as I am aware, she did not cry again. My mother told me how brave her friend was, and how we had to admire her for bringing up her family all alone. Was it from that memory that I formed my attitude to how widows ought to act? I do not know, but it does fit my picture. I felt happy as a child to be living next door to a widow like that. She was a kind person and my mother loved her. They were close friends. I had no awareness of the loneliness and agony of her widowhood.

Something to do

During your life's journey, you will have gathered much which will be an asset to you as you stand by those who mourn. You might also be conscious that you have accumulated quite a pile of 'logs'—those less helpful attitudes and feelings which get in the the way when you try to understand someone else's grief situation. I invite you to use the following questions to help you consider this, or better still, ask a close friend to do it along with you. Chat it through together. If you are using the book in a group, I suggest that you think things through for yourself first of all, and then divide the group into twos or threes for the sharing.

Your purpose in thinking this through will be to see how much you may be influenced by the experiences of death and grieving you have had in the past. The questions are designed to help you look at what took place when you were too young to understand the significance of what was happening around you and how your early exposure to grief could be affecting your effectiveness in this area of pastoral care today.

An Exercise

For you to think through by yourself and then, perhaps, to share with others.

1. *Which are your earliest memories of bereavement, or of people who were mourning?*
    a) *What actually happened, and how did you come to know about it?*
    b) *How old would you be at the time?*
    c) *At that age, how well would you reckon you would be able to understand what was happening?*
    d) *How did the people around you react in that situation?*
    e) *How did you react to their ways of grieving?*
    f) *What do you think you picked up at that age, about death, and about how to mourn?*
    g) *Do you think any of your current attitudes to the dying or the bereaved are influenced by what happened so long ago?*
    h) *If your answer to (g) is 'yes', what will you need to re-examine now that you have the resources to do this?*
2. *Which experiences from the rest of your life, have helped mould your thoughts, feelings and attitudes about loss, to what they are today?*
3. *How does your faith influence your current attitude to death and bereavement?*

4. *What is it about this subject, that makes you want to know more about it?*

When you have given some thought to these questions you will have written your own introduction to the learning you will discover through this book.

Take Care!

As a teacher, I am very conscious of the drawbacks to learning a subject like pastoral care from a book. The words on a page cannot take care of their readers as a teacher can of the people she sees around her in a class of adults learning together. When I am teaching, I can see if someone in my class has tears in his eyes or is looking tearful or bewildered as an old memory brings back strong feelings. Do take care of yourself!

If at any time you feel you need help, find someone to support you. Your Christian community might have someone trained in counselling who will listen and then pray with you. Remember that the best comforters are often those who have known their own need for support and have been open to receive this from others.

CHAPTER THREE

Change is rough

God said, 'I will lead my blind people by roads they have never travelled. I will turn their darkness into light, and will make rough country smooth before them. These are my promises and I will keep them without fail.'

Isaiah 42 : 16 (G N B)

Modern life is full of change and some changes can be very rough to live through. Each change, for each person, is a unique blend of gain and loss. Some are dramatic and traumatic; others are barely noticed.

For instance, some people find the change from being single to being married, an easy and happy one.

It was very different for Serena, a capable professional woman in her mid-forties who had her own flat exactly as she wanted it. For years she had to please no-one but herself in her private life. Serena married a man who was divorced and still supporting his former wife and two daughters from his income. He moved into her flat.

Courtship had been a joy to them both. Their relationship had brought a new dimension to the lives they had been living before they met. But after a few weeks of marriage, Serena's frustration level was at a peak. She felt that her new husband had invaded her space. His clothes were strewn everywhere. When he tidied up, he did not put things back where she had always kept them. She found it difficult to get a good night's sleep because she could not get used to sharing a bed . . . and he snored! He had managed to survive on his own while his divorce was being processed so why should he expect her to stop whatever she was doing to make a meal for *him* if he came in late? She felt taken over by his body, his needs, even his whims . . . She was being used!

In Hospital

Another change which can be a totally contrasting experience for two different people is that of being taken into hospital. Imagine a happy four year old from a loving family, feeling so ill that his mother cannot make him feel better. Without warning he is whisked off to be surrounded by white-coated, masked medical staff, who jab him with needles. All his normal security is gone. Traces of this trauma could well last into his adult life.

Contrast that with the experience of an elderly widower, struggling since the death of his wife, trying to cook for himself, getting used to living alone, battling against feeling that he mattered to no-one. He had a dizzy turn, fell, and broke his leg badly. A spell in hospital made him feel the centre of attention again. He suffered no deprivation till he was discharged as fit to resume his lonely life again.

Life is full of change; some of it predictable and prepared for, some sudden and shocking. Most changes have some element of loss for some people. Many changes have so much loss that they are accompanied by severe deprivation—physical, psychological, emotional, spiritual—sometimes by deprivation of all that seems to make life meaningful.

Stop! Think for yourself for a few minutes about the changes life brings.

An Exercise

Start from the very first change that most people experience—the change from the security of the womb, which comes at birth—and then note down some of the other changes an average person can expect to encounter on life's journey, right through to old age and death.

> eg *birth*
> *being weaned*
> *arrival of a new brother or sister*
> *beginning nursery school . . .*

Were you surprised at the length of your list?

Each time you travel by bus, go to church, or engage in countless everyday activities, you will be rubbing shoulders with people who are trying to cope with change. Some of these will be suffering from the intense deprivation which follows change that involves major loss.

Recovering from this deprivation can take a long time—even years of readjustment. Some carry a sense of acute deprivation till their life's end. For most people, adjustment takes place gradually, and life eventually assumes new meaning and purpose. Some kind of balance is regained and positive energy for living and loving is once again available.

Loss can leave a person drained of energy

In the time of acute deprivation which comes from major loss, it can seem as if no positive energy is coming in to re-charge our emotional batteries. It feels as if someone has pulled out a plug, disconnecting us from everything that has given life meaning and purpose. We can feel physically, emotionally and spiritually drained, with no reserves for our own use and nothing to give to others. In this highly vulnerable position, our initial reaction can be to withdraw into whatever shell we can pull around our heads rather than risk any openness and invite further hurt.

Frances

A social worker called one day on a young woman named Frances. Her department had been alerted by a neighbour who was concerned about the woman's three children being allowed, as she said, 'to run wild at all hours'. The social worker found a depressed and very lonely young mother whose husband had gone off with another girl from that district. She was having to suffer, not only the loss of her husband and the father of her children, but loss of friendship with neighbours who did not want to be involved in a scandal.

People were acting as if Frances did not exist. She was getting no positive energy for her emotional batteries. Without realising what she was doing, she had been seeking some negative attention, since that was infinitely better than the feeling that she mattered to no-one. She had little motivation for caring for her children. She knew they would annoy the neighbours but did nothing to stop them. And getting nothing from her, the children were naughty and difficult to handle. They needed her attention. Instead of being able to deal with their behaviour, Frances looked on it as proof that she was not only a failure as a wife, but also as a mother.

Before all this, Frances had been a wife and mother who cared about her husband and children and whose sense of self-worth was greatly linked to being needed by them and to receiving from them, the positive energy for the life she lived. Her relationship with her husband had not caused her undue concern. She had been totally unprepared for her husband's desertion. The visit from the social worker, was the first indication Frances had had for six weeks that someone cared. She was gently faced with the reality of how much she mattered to her children. Gradually, because she was being cared for, she was able to care for them again.

The social worker contacted another woman who had been through a similar experience a few years before, who willingly gave Frances a great deal of support. She had learned to listen to and confront any destructive self-pity. She became a sign of hope for Frances. With her help, Frances faced up to the possibility of her husband not returning home. Eventually she began to build meaning into her life without him.

Each loss feels unique to the one who sustains it. Some losses seem to leave mourners drained of the will to begin the process of readjustment until something happens to show that someone cares.

Destructive Energy

In contrast to that, loss can bring an enormous build-up of negative energy and that can create havoc for existing relationships. So further loss becomes possible.

Serena

Earlier in this chapter I mentioned Serena, the woman who had been single, till, in her mid-forties, she married Simon. About six weeks after the wedding, her frustration level 'peaked'. Their honeymoon seemed like a far-off dream. It had been wonderful but it was in the past. The present seemed to have little to commend it.

Serena felt very tired—tired through lack of sleep, tense from bottling up frustration. She was far too proud to confide in her friends that she was wondering if her marriage had been a mistake. She would not tell Simon how miserably trapped and guilty she felt. She wished she had thought more about the effects of bringing him into her flat to live there. She was much too used to living on her own. Being in love, she had imagined that everything would work out. He was so happy again—how would he react to discovering that his new wife wished she had never married him when he had already been through the pain of a divorce? No! She could not do that to him.

The confused jumble of her thoughts and feelings churned inside as she came home from work one evening. She made the meal and Simon ate it cheerfully, apparently oblivious of the fact that she was contributing almost nothing to the meal-time conversation. After it was over, she carried the dishes to the sink. Simon went off in the opposite direction. 'He's using me!' she thought angrily. 'I've done all the shopping, all the cooking, and now I've to wash and dry the dishes while he's off on some other ploy!'

Soft, romantic music began to drift through the loudspeaker system, in complete contrast to her mood. She bristled, and plunged her hands into the hot, soapy dish-water. Suddenly she felt Simon's arms around her, and a whisper in her ear, 'Leave these! Come on. I want you!' That did it! Serena's self-control snapped. She straightened up, whirled round, and slapped her soapy hand across his face. 'Get out of my house!' she shrieked.

Their marriage survived.

It was about eighteen months before Serena had made the necessary adjustment, and could say—and feel—that being married to Simon was even better than being happily single. Some of her adjustments came about so gradually that she barely noticed them. Some were so major that they seemed to require a crisis to start them off. That first fight had forced her to see that she could not carry that build-up of frustration inside without seriously affecting her relationship with Simon.

After she had screamed out her resentment and fear, she had burst into tears of humiliation. It was a couple of hours later that Simon managed to risk telling her that his putting his arms around her at the sink, while playing dreamy music, had been his way of saying, 'Something is making you unhappy. I want to make you as happy as I can. Come and relax and tell me what's wrong.'

Over the months, Serena grew able to tell Simon how she felt instead of bottling everything inside her till it burst out, rejecting and hurting. Simon, too began to ask her directly what was wrong when he noticed her withdrawing into herself. One weekend Simon went off to a residential conference. Serena could not get to sleep. She felt cold. Then she realised that she had grown so used to sleeping with Simon that it felt strange not to have him there.

One of the worst things that Serena had had to face was her feeling that Simon had invaded her space. During a chance conversation with a friend who was converting her daughter's bedroom into a sewing room for herself now that the girl had left home, Serena hit on the idea of making the box room in her flat *her* place, where she could read or sew when Simon wanted to watch a Western on television. Having her own space worked wonders for her psychologically, although in practice she rarely went there when Simon was in.

The adjustments took their own course, with hurt and painful growing for both. Their relationship became richer than ever it had been in the romantic haze of their honeymoon. Serena lost the life she had before but the new life she shared was worth all the hard work of readjustment.

Worksheet

I now invite you to work out how you have adjusted to a major change in your life which involved losses.

Here is Serena's experience:

What was the change that triggered off the losses for you?	
It was my marriage and Simon moving in with me to the flat where I had lived independently before that.	

What did you lose?	*How are you getting on with readjustment?*
My privacy	*I've been slowly learning to share, and enjoy it. I know what I must share and what is O.K. to keep to myself.*
Physical space	*A gradual adjustment. Great help when I made the boxroom into 'my' place.*
Sleep	*Got used to sleeping with Simon. Now I sleep best when he's beside me.*
Orderliness	*Still have not adjusted to Simon's untidiness—but he's more considerate now. Doesn't make me angry as it used to.*
Being able to consider only myself in my private life.	*Gradually have grown used to not being so selfish! Now I quite enjoy the give and take of partnership. Still annoys me if Simon makes a decision for both of us.*

Now work on your loss situation:

1. *First, select a change which triggered off losses for you. It could be the breaking of a relationship, the fading of a dream, moving house, losing part of your body, experiencing the loss or deterioration of a faculty, or whatever has been important for you.*

Take care of yourself. Do not chose to work on any major change you have had within the past year. It often takes longer than that fully to readjust, and to recharge your batteries for living life creatively once more.

2. *Now, list all the significant things you lost when that major change took place—all the big and little things that had been meaningful to you in your lifestyle before the change and that had kept your batteries charged.*

3. *Finally, write beside each one of these, what you have put in its place as being equally significant to you now.*

Spaces to fill

If you can write something beside each item then you have recovered from the losses and adjusted well to your new life. There may, however, be some spaces you will never fill.

If you discover that you have some blanks which could be filled if you worked at them, plan to do so. Fill them as soon as you can.

Your loss situation

What was the change that triggered off the losses for you?	
What did you lose?	How are you getting on with your readjustment?

Now that you have thought through a personal change, and how you have been working to readjust your life since then, it will be easier for you to understand how long it might take other people to recover from their losses. Remember that recovery is normal.

CHAPTER FOUR

Facing change

Sharing experiences can help others prepare for change

Kirsten and Ken had prepared in every way they could think of for the birth of their first child, but it had not occurred to them to talk through how it might affect their own relationship. After the excitement of the birth of their son, Ken began to feel more and more excluded from the rosy glow that surrounded Kirsten and the baby. Kirsten's emotional batteries were overflowing with the fulfilment of motherhood but when Ken came home from work it was either to be told 'Sshh. Don't waken him!' or 'I'm having a job to settle him. Haven't had any time to get a meal for us.'

Kirsten was giving all she had to their son. Nothing seemed to be left over for Ken. He felt deeply hurt and cheated, and very insecure when he handled his son, because he did this so rarely. He felt he was not needed and then that he was not even wanted. He began to work late or go to the pub before he came home at night.

One of Ken's friends at the pub noticed how withdrawn he seemed to be. 'What's up with you?' was all he needed to say for Ken to launch into a tale of self-pity. After listening to him for a few minutes, he interrupted him. "Look here, mate. It's not me you should be saying all this to. It's your wife.' When Ken tried to tell Kirsten how he felt, she was very defensive. She claimed that he had shown no interest in the baby, nor in her, since the birth. They fought. Kirsten cried. But they had begun to talk again. Kirsten was appalled when she understood how her possessiveness had pushed Ken away, robbing him of the experience of feeling like a father.

Some of Ken and Kirsten's friends had been through a similar time, but it had not occurred to them to pass on something of their experience to the couple. Talking about how things might be in the middle of a major change in life is not, of couse, a guarantee that the pain of the change will be avoided! What it can mean is that when the pain comes, it does not take you by surprise. With some help, they could have realised that they were in for a time of change when they would both have to adjust. They needed to try to understand and support each other.

So often, too, in the midst of a crisis, all those caught up in it are over-tired and under unusual strain. At times like these, few people stand back and take time to think how it might be for the others involved with them or make allowances for the effects of strain on themselves and others. It is possible to help others face expected change even if the helper has had no previous experience of that same change, in his or her own life. What is needed is sufficient imagination to sense where pain might come for others and enough concern to invite them to look ahead and prepare themselves.

Two contrasting attempts to help others face change

Norman was the pastor of a very small congregation. After church one day the Jones family came to tell him they were moving to London. Norman felt a sense of personal loss. He took out his diary and fixed an evening when he could visit them before they left. To prepare himself for the visit, Norman prayerfully listed the changes he imagined the Jones family would be facing when they moved. During his visit he went over these changes one by one, asking them gently of their plans for looking after themselves in each time of change.

For most of the things Norman mentioned, the Jones family

had a response that they had already thought through, but in some areas Norman's caring conversation sparked off ideas they might never have had without his stimulation.

Norman had not thought for the Jones family *how* they should take care of themselves. He had invited them to do their own thinking.

Contrast Norman's pastoral insight with the lack of sensitivity shown by Joan's friend. Within three years of marriage, Joan had three children. Her husband had not wanted her to take a job as the children grew up. Joan's daughter was married the year her twin brothers were due to leave home for university two hundred miles away.

Joan's friend was anxious about her. She knew that Joan was about to experience an 'empty nest' with very little to keep her occupied. So she thought through what Joan ought to do.

Friend: I've been thinking, Joan, that it's time you had a life of your own. Your sons have wound you round their little fingers.

Joan: Oh, believe me, I'm quite happy with what I do for them. They don't demand. I give!

Friend: Well, I'm going to an evening class on modern history each Wednesday, and I think it would do you the world of good to come along with me.

Joan: Actually, I've never been particularly keen on history.

Friend: Well, have you ever thought of a Cordon Bleu cookery class? I wouldn't mind fitting that in if you would prefer it.

Joan: Really, I don't feel I need to reach that standard. My family enjoys simple cooking of good food, and that's what I like to give them.

Friend: I've been flicking through the literature for the Open University, and it looks fascinating! If you would be interested. I'd give up all thought of evening courses and go into that wholeheartedly, if you would do it along with me.

Joan: But I already have a degree that I've barely used!

Friend: That's what I mean! Things have changed so much since we were students that you'd probably not be able to get a job when the family leaves unless you've done some recent study.

Joan: But who's talking about a job? Just what are you getting at? I'm beginning to feel uncomfortable with this conversation. . . .

An Exercise

For you to think through by yourself, or with others.

Do NOT think up a solution to Joan's problem for her! Instead think up a question you might ask Joan if you were her friend, which could invite her to begin to think through the challenge of her 'empty nest' situation for herself.

CHAPTER FIVE

Cries for help

I kept quiet, not saying a word,
not even about anything good!

But my suffering only grew worse,
and I was overcome with anxiety.

The more I thought, the more troubled I became . . .'
                                        Psalm 39 : 2, 3 (GNB)

A belief that people are of infinite value implies that when
they need help, they should get it. When a human personality
needs attention, it asks for attention in one way or another. In
our culture, and perhaps most markedly in our Christian
culture, it is not always acceptable for people to talk openly
about their needs and to have them openly met once they are
beyond childhood. As we grow up, we learn to ask indirectly
for what we need.

Imagine a woman who is very tired. Instead of saying
directly, 'I would love a cup of tea. Will you make me one,
please? I'm feeling very tired,' she is likely to sit down heavily,
with a sigh, hoping that someone will notice and respond: 'You
sound *so* weary. Sit there till I make you a nice cup of tea.'
Our society tends to frown on the first way of asking but
applaud the second.

Have you ever suspected that a gift you had received was a
veiled bribe to get attention? When people ask indirectly, those
who pick up the underlying message can feel used and
manipulated. We can all use underhand ways of relating to

others to inveigle them into meeting our needs. Sometimes we choose to manipulate. At other times, we can be unaware of our reasons for producing certain behaviour. But, whether or not we are doing it consciously, we are seeking attention . . . and we are needy people. Only God knows our needs before we tell him about them. Others don't!

At the news of a death, an accident, a redundancy, or a sudden severe illness, friends, relatives and neighbours often gather in large numbers with a great deal of loving attention in the form of practical help, kind words, and a sharing of their time. Those most concerned with the loss are generally dazed with shock at that point and can barely be conscious of what is going on around them. They can have the feeling of being greatly upheld by the loving concern of others although details go unnoticed. But at the time when neighbourly concern has dwindled, the emptiness left can be very sore. It can be so severe as to trigger off the most painful part of grieving.

Emotional Starvation

One way to understand why the personality of the grieving person appears to alter so radically during this phase, is to liken it to an emotional starvation—intense deprivation—so great that logical, rational thought is temporarily suspended in a desperate bid to have overwhelming needs met.

A young widow was visited after the funeral by one of her late husband's colleagues, who had come to offer the condolences of the staff. Later, she was deeply ashamed and bewildered at her behaviour that evening. She had begun to cry, and he had responded by putting his arms around her. The feeling of being held close was so good. It was all she wanted and needed. Without asking, here were her needs being met. She relaxed against his body, feeling that as long as he held her, the pain and desolation would be kept at bay.

Looking back at the visit, the man also felt confused and ashamed. His heart had gone out to her when she had cried. He wanted to protect her. Then he felt her snuggling against him. He did not think to check out his understanding of her needs. Her closeness aroused him and he had carried her to bed.

He realised later that she had not wanted that.

A man who had been at the top of his professional career in early middle age and who was normally quiet and unassuming in company, was made redundant without warning. He began to go out drinking. The more he drank, the more he talked, boring any who would listen with exaggerated stories of his skills at his past job. He badly needed to know that he still mattered. His desperate attempt to get this reassurance failed.

An elderly woman had devotedly nursed an ailing husband for more than twenty years. When he died, the emptiness left by the loss of being so intensely needed became intolerable to her. Too quickly she discovered a frail neighbour and transferred to her all the loving energy she had been pouring out on her husband. She nursed her for two years until the neighbour's doctor took her into permanent psychiatric care.

When her neighbour was taken away she still had not worked through her grief for her husband. She had merely suspended it through busy-ness. She had not adjusted to not being needed. She was two years older, much more physically exhausted than at the time of her husband's death and much less fit to face readjustment.

Psychosomatic Illness

Perhaps the most distressing result of needs not being openly acknowledged and met is seen when the human body translates the need for attention into psychosomatic illness or complaint.

In British society, the doctor's surgery is freely available. It can be the one place where many feel they can legitimately request attention and human touch. Grieving people, suffering from any form of loss, crave loving understanding in the midst of their painful deprivation. It sometimes follows therefore that their bodies provide them with valid grounds for seeking what they need.

In 1968, research was published examining the health of widows in the year following bereavement.* The researchers made a list of psychosomatic grief reactions found in the widows they studied. These were physical symptoms which the widows reported to doctors in excess of the same symptoms reported by matched control groups of women. Recorded in this were migraine, headache, dizziness, fainting spells, blurred vision, facial pain, skin rashes, excessive sweating, indigestion, difficulty in swallowing, peptic ulceration, colitis, vomiting, excessive appetite, anorexia, weight gain, menorrhagia, palpitations, chest pain, dyspnoea, asthma, frequent infections, general aching, neoplastic growth and diabetes mellitus.

Research along similar lines is presently being carried out amongst those who have lost employment in the current economic crisis, as it is believed that this loss may have a similar effect on health.

Stress can build up after a loss

A major loss in the life of any person is often followed by several other losses, each of which can bring its own stress.

Take the case of John, sixty-eight at his wife's death. His children decided that their father could not cope on his own. He should come to live with each one of them in turn. John was still dazed by his loss and it felt good to be looked after for a while. It was not long before John realised that he had lost, not only his wife, but his home, his garden, his independence, his choice of what to eat, and when to eat it, his choice

* 'The Health of Widows in the Year following Bereavement.' Maddison, D. and Viola, A. *Journal of Psychosomatic Research*, 1968.

to wave goodbye to his boisterous grandchildren till their next visit. He had also lost the friends and status he had enjoyed in his village.

Of course, the greatest loss was that of his day-to-day relationship with his wife but in many ways he felt he might have adapted to that loss much more quickly, if he had not had to cope with all the other losses too. He could have made a new and independent life in his familiar environment and enjoyed the occasional visit to each of his children's families. Now he felt helpless, and a burden to the younger generations.

An Exercise

For you to think through by yourself, or with others

Do you belong to an organisation or live in a community where employees are given houses for as long as they continue in a particular job? (eg the clergy, armed forces personnel, police) If you do, you might like to list all the losses that can fall on dependents of the employee, if he or she retires, is made redundant, falls seriously ill or dies.

Here is a table compiled by Drs Thomas Holmes and Richard Rache of the Washington Medical School in America. This should help you assess the possible effect of the kind of losses you have listed, on those who sustain them. (Scores given beside each crisis can be added up to give a total 'stress level' score.)

Those whose score at any one time reaches above 160 have a high probability of their health being affected by the stress involved in loss. Yet people react differently to stress. Some tested on this scale who scored over 400 showed no sign of ill-health!

Death of husband or wife	100	Large mortgage taken out	31
Divorce	73	Child leaves home	29
Marital separation	65	In-laws problem	29
Jail sentence	63	Major personal achievement realised	28
Death of close member of family	63	Wife starts or stops work	26
Illness or injury	53	Starting or leaving school	26
Marriage	50	Change in living conditions	25
Loss of job	47	Trouble with employer	23
Retirement	45	Change in residence	20
Health problem of close family	44	Change in recreation	19
Pregnancy	40	Small mortgage or bank loan	17
Sex problems	39	Change in sleeping habits	16
Major change at work	39	Change in family get-togethers	15
Change of financial status	38	Change in eating habits	15
Death of a close friend	37	Christmas	12
Increase in marital arguments	35	Minor violation of law	11

(*This list was published in the 'Sunday Express Magazine', October 4, 1981.*)

Scoring

Here is what Holmes and Rache claimed for their scoring:

Score under 150: The person is living a stable, safe way of life and is less prone to illness and accident than most other people.

Score 150–200: The chance of a person having a health or safety problem has risen to 37%.

Score 200–300: This person is just as likely (51%) to have a health or safety problem as not.

Score over 300: BEWARE! This person has a 79% health or safety problem.

Another Exercise

For you to think through by yourself or with others

1. Look at the Stress Level Table above.

a) *What do you think of the scores suggested? Any you would wish to alter?*

b) *Add up the score of your current stress level.*

c) *If you are experiencing enough stress to have scored 200 or more, what can you do to reduce this? Do it!*

2. *Earlier in this chapter you were invited to make a list of possible losses particular persons might face on losing their home:*

a) *Put beside each item, the suggested score.*

b) *If you have some on your list which do not appear on the Table, judge for yourself an appropriate score for that loss, and note it.*

c) *Calculate the score for that person's stress level.*

d) *If you are in a group of people (eg a church) who are responsible now and then for asking people to leave a tied house, is there any way you could reduce the possible stress level involved for them to a minimum?*

3. *Have some fun making up another table in complete contrast to the Stress Level Table. This time, make it a table where you list all the things you can think of that reduce stress and give each one of these a score out of a hundred.*

Here are a few to start you off:

Having someone who loves and supports you
Having someone who will listen to you
Feeling yourself in God's presence
Complete physical relaxation
Taking strenuous physical exercise . . .

and so on.

What score would you give to these?

CHAPTER SIX

The grief process

*'He sets the time for sorrow and the time for joy,
the time for mourning and the time for dancing.'*
                                        Eccles. 3 : 4 (GNB)

In order to recover from any loss, grief must be faced and
worked through. Grieving is a natural process. Moving through
it, people can grow towards a fulfilling life without whatever
they have had to leave behind. In grieving, a person moves
through several stages of readjustment. Looking back he or
she can view it as a total process of growth.

I look back to August 1968 when I set off alone to study in
the USA. I had no idea that I would be facing any grief
process. I expected to miss friends and family but I was excited
at the prospect of all that lay ahead.

The first stage I lived through was wonderful. I spent three
weeks with a family in a wealthy suburb of New York,
sightseeing, enjoying a high standard of living, meeting new
people and new ideas. I felt elated.

Then I moved to Chicago, arriving there shortly after riots
where my now-fellow students had clashed with the police.
Blacks were militant and, for the first time in my life I was
living in an area with a predominantly black population. I
became frightened. I felt there was nobody I could trust. I
shut myself in my study bedroom when not attending classes
and I grew depressed. I had never experienced feelings like
the ones that seemed to swamp me. Gradually my fellow

students reached out to me and I was able to begin to relate to them, but the area of trust in others which had never consciously worried me back home was something I was having to relearn. It was a painfully slow process with many set-backs. Eventually I was able to enjoy life there, and open myself up to the dramatic experiences all around me. I could evaluate them for myself, accepting some and rejecting others. I had grown in all kinds of ways.

If I was to map out the stages of my grief process in adjusting to life in the States, they would be:

1. Elation
2. Fear and depression
3. Painful orientation to a new way of life
4. Happy participation in the new life

When the time came, I found it very difficult to go home and settle down again. That, in fact, was another grief process.

Unemployment

During 1982 there was a series of broadcasts on Radio Scotland on unemployment. One outlined possible stages of reaction to long-term unemployment. During the programme I made the following notes.

Stage one DENIAL
  'Great! A holiday, plus all this redundancy pay! Let's go to Spain for two weeks: buy a video recorder: redecorate the whole house.
    Feels great. Spirits high. Energy output high.

Stage two, GRADUALLY INCREASING DISTRESS
  Application after job application leads to nothing. Sometimes not even an acknowledgement.
    'I don't deserve this.'
    Restlessness: cannot relax: sleeplessness: headaches and

other general aches and pains: digestive upsets: sense of personal worthlessness creeps in: loses temper easily—especially at home. May lead to visits to the GP resulting in increase in use of drugs. Increase in alcohol consumption, smoking and gambling: marital problems: violence—occasionally murder.

Stage three, BECOMES BROKEN AND RESIGNED
  No longer actively seeks a job. Tends to stay in—and in bed. Stares out of the window. Concentration to read or watch TV gone.
    Self-esteem at rock-bottom. Lethargic. Feels suicidal.
    Likelihood of clinical depression; cardio-vascular trouble; cirrhosis of the liver.

Not everyone reaches stage three. Some lucky ones find new jobs. Some are motivated and able to set up in self-employment. Some find fulfillment in voluntary work or in developing a hobby or skill. But in a time of mass unemployment, whole towns are affected by one industry or firm closing down. Thus hundreds of redundant workers may reach stage three together with a devastating effect on the physical, psychological and spiritual health of the whole community.

An Exercise

For you to think through by yourself or with others.
  Select a major loss you have worked through.
  Write down the stages you went through during that experience.
  If you are in a group, share this with the others and learn from theirs.

The Grief Process

Ancient cultures knew a great deal about what we now call 'The Grief Process'. Built into their traditions were ceremonies to be acted out at the actual death, while others marked the passage of time at specified intervals after that. Many had a special ritual to be observed on the first anniversary. So, in the close-knit community of tribal life, readjustment to loss was being helped centuries before modern researchers worked to rediscover this old knowledge.

Modern scientific documentation on the effects of major loss on the average human personality was greatly helped by a follow-up study done in the USA. Many families were bereaved in Boston as a result of a fire at a nightclub named 'Coconut Grove'. Over a period, the bereaved families were supported and counselled and their reactions recorded. Subsequently the findings were written up in an article by Dr Erich Lindemann, Professor of Psychiatry at Harvard. His article was entitled *Symptomatology and Management of Acute Grief* and it was published in the *American Journal of Psychiatry*, September 1944. In it, for the first time, possible stages in the grief process were spelled out. He also wrote of the differences between normal grief reactions and abnormal or morbid grief. He stressed the necessity for helping bereaved persons work through their grief. In his own words, this help was to enable a mourner 'to extricate himself from the bondage to the deceased and find new patterns of rewarding interaction'.

Each grieving person is unique. Each takes his or her own time to grow through the various stages. Some appear to miss out some stages altogether. Some seem to have moved on to the next stage and then to regress to one they have already been through. A few seem to have little motivation for moving on through the whole process. These appear to need to remain at a stage which gives them a particular form of attention. A few stick so thoroughly at one stage that they have to be taken into long-term institutional care. Some stay at one stage for years, then something triggers off their grief, and within a few hours, or even minutes, they may complete the whole process in one great catharsis.

The Stages of Grief

Yorick Spiegel, in his book *The Grief Process* (published by SCM Press) suggests that beareaved people grow through the four stages listed below. Beside each is his suggestion of the average time this takes.*

1. SHOCK	*From a few minutes to two days*
2. CONTROL	*From around three to seven days— usually till after the funeral*
3. REGRESSION	*Usually around three to six months*
4. ADAPTATION	*From six months to one year*

In fact, any major loss is likely to set a very similar grief process in motion. Divorce or separation from any close partner, redundancy or enforced retirement, the process of facing one's own dying . . . There are many acute grief situations likely to echo this pattern.

---

* Dr. Colin Murray Parkes, a specialist on bereavement, suggests the recovery takes up to two years.

CHAPTER SEVEN

Shock

The grief process begins with shock—the reaction triggered off at the news of a significant and generally unexpected loss. *Shock is a person's whole being shouting 'NO!'*

Cathy was ten years old and her cat was a very close and special friend. The family noticed that his digestive system was out of sorts, so Cathy's mother took Sebastian to the vet during school hours. He discovered the cat had leukemia and had better be put to sleep right away. And so she arrived home with the cat's lifeless form in his basket.

Cathy rushed home from school for news of the visit to the vet. Her mother started to tell her what had happened. As soon as Cathy realised the truth, her hands flew to cover her ears and she screamed, 'I don't want to hear! I don't want to hear!' Sensing that Cathy ought to say goodbye to her cat, her mother went to open the cat's basket. 'No! I don't want to see!' she yelled. Her screaming continued for a full ten minutes.

'No. I don't believe it!' is the normal response to hearing bad news. Sometimes the sense of disbelief fades in and out of a mourner's consciousness for days. In the face of such a psychological blow, all the personality can do is to protect itself against something immensely threatening to the fragile shell of meaning that holds its world together.

Shock reactions are unpredictable

One of the many unenviable tasks of the police force is to take news of a fatal accident to the next-of-kin of those killed.

They encounter shock reactions. Some receive the news in stunned silence: some scream hysterically: some refuse to believe that the news is being delivered to the correct address: some faint: some attack the officer who brings the news: some accept the news so calmly that they seem not to have understood.

One young officer had to break to a mother that her six-year-old son had been run over. He also had a son of that age and had begun to imagine how he would have felt in her place. But when told, what had happened her words to him were: 'Did you get his clothes? I've another five. They'll do the next one.' The policeman's reaction was that *he* wanted to slap her on the face!

Someone in shock does not stop to consider 'What will people think of me if I faint/punch/scream?' The reaction is immediate and any thinking about the effect of that reaction on others will come later—if, in fact, it comes at all. It will probably not be recalled later.

A person in shock can be out of touch with the normal ability people have to look after themselves. Someone in shock might sit down in stunned silence and do nothing till the shock wears off. In that state, he or she will probably be unaware of others in the room. On the other hand, some people in shock make quick, hysterical decisions, like running across a busy road without first checking the traffic flow, driving recklessly, attacking another with a knife, or saying hurtful words he or she would ordinarily not dream of saying.

Very occasionally people in shock commit suicide.

A person in shock should not be alone

If you have to convey bad news, make sure, if it is at all possible, that you do it face-to-face. If you are there you can keep an eye on the shocked person. If you have to pass on bad news by telephone, try to discover if there are others around the person you are phoning who can be with him or her for a while.

Recently I heard of a hospital which runs a 'Good Neighbour' scheme, where volunteers from the neighbourhood are trained to be with others—often complete strangers to themselves—after the doctor gives the news of the death of a relative. The Good Neighbour will stay with the relatives in a little private room in the hospital for a time and then will be responsible for taking them to their own home and calling in a friend or neighbour to be around the bereaved for a while afterwards.

Unfortunately there are many incidents where bad news is received and there is no provision made for looking after the person in shock. Factory workers have been told that their factory is to be closed down and then have been sent back to work with dangerous machinery. Spouses have been told in the doctor's waiting room that their partner has terminal cancer and then have had to drive home.

Shock can block off normal listening and remembering

Doctors are human beings. They dread giving any kind of suffering to their patients and this includes giving bad news.

Muriel was a young doctor who worked in an Oncology Unit in a city hospital. She firmly believed that her patients deserved to be told the truth about what was wrong with them. She believed that only when they understood what might lie ahead were they able to give her the guidance she needed to do what was best for them. Because she was so sensitive and concerned about her patients, she used to explain to them, in as kindly a manner as possible, that they had cancer. Thinking to cushion the blow, she would, almost immediately, launch into an explanation of possible treatments and the results which could be expected from them. It took her a long time to realise that most of her patients sat there, letting her talk, but taking in virtually nothing of what she was pouring over their dazed consciousness. Eventually she learned to give them the bad news, and then to be with them—often saying nothing but available for what they wanted and needed from her.

Before she left, she would promise to return the following day to discuss possible treatments. Meantime, she would alert the nursing staff to keep a close eye on the patient, and to provide a listening ear if it was needed.

If you have to convey bad news, and at the same time, have to pass on information:

1. *Write the information down, and leave it to be re-read later or*
2. *Visit again later on, or the following day with, 'Thought I'd call in again to see if there's anything you'd like to check up on, now that you've had time to think.'*
3. *If you have to give bad news by phone, follow it up with a letter giving the information over again, or phone again the following day to find out how the person is, and to check that the information has been heard accurately.*

Only when people come out of shock do they realise that there were questions they ought to have asked but were too stunned to do so. They can also feel very guilty if they remember being given information but cannot recall it in detail. If the person who conveyed the news was an authority figure for them, they may not want to contact him or her to get the information repeated to them. On the other hand, they could be unaware of the fact that the person tried to convey information to them that they did not hear. In such a circumstance, they will not know that they should take steps to obtain further information. Back-up services are therefore required for this kind of situation. Always leave the door open for the correction of misunderstandings or wrong information.

Shock is part of the natural healing process in grief

Although for the onlooker, a shock reaction in another person may seem odd or even frightening, that particular way

of reacting will be what that personality needs to do for pro-
tection at that moment. He or she will not have made any
conscious decision about what to do. It will have taken place
automatically. Do not interfere unless the automatic reaction
of the person is to do something harmful. Do not, for instance,
insist that the person sits still if he or she wishes to be active.
Just make sure that there is somebody around who is not also
in shock and who can do whatever is appropriate to keep the
one in shock from any harm.

The obvious effects of shock may be over in a few seconds,
and the person who has received bad news can move very
swiftly into the control phase of grief. You will know this has
happened when the shocked person shows signs of being aware
of other people and of what these others might be feeling and
thinking. Words like, 'What must you be thinking of me?' or
'I must wear black. My father would like that' or 'Does George
know yet?' indicate that shock is receding.

It is still advisable to have someone around, however, unless
at this stage the grieving person chooses to be left alone. There
are some people who much prefer to be alone to try to pull
themselves together so unless you have any reason to suspect
that it is not safe to leave, do respect their wishes in this
matter. They will know what they have to do to look after
themselves.

Shock is a natural temporary anaesthetic

With a shock reaction, the brain cushions itself from feeling
the full effect of the pain the loss brings. But this can only be
a temporary measure. If the effects of shock seem too long in
wearing off, do not hesitate to call a doctor, because the
shocked person might well need medical attention.

The day after a shock occurs, and often for much longer
than a day, the person concerned will feel completely drained
and exhausted. Concentration is likely to be poor, and appetite
small. Often the digestive system has been knocked off bal-

ance—but since these occur in the control stage, I will leave them for a fuller treatment in the next chapter.

Shock may not be most severe at the time of death

Most deaths in our society today are not sudden: many die as the result of a period of illness whether long or short, or of old age. Because of this, the shock phase can be most acute, not on learning the news of the actual death, but rather at the news that the illness might prove fatal, or when a change for the worse is seen in the ill or elderly person.

Many elderly people now have such healthy bodies that the first bad signs of deterioration are seen in the mind and not in their physical health. Shock can take place for the relatives at the discovery of some piece of behaviour that seems completely out of character. Those close to the person in that condition can sense the beginning of the end of the personality as they have known it. The relationship they have had together up until that point begins to alter radically and can die long before the body has ceased to function. Thus distress can be protracted and can be less easily dealt with than if the death of the body had occurred. The loss of the relationship will be mourned, perhaps years before the body is buried.

Sometimes death can be much more of a relief than a shock to relatives and friends. An illness, whether physical or mental, can have gone on for so long that the grief process can have been worked right through before death finally occurs, leaving only a period of readjustment rather than a time of mourning. But for many people, the death of someone who has been close to them is a shock whenever it happens. This is so even if it has been longed and prayed for, and even if it has been expected. Death is the end of the kind of relationship one person can have with another in this life whether that relationship has been good, bad or indifferent.

An Exercise

For personal reflection and/or group sharing

1. *Think back to a time when you received bad news. How did you react to the news?*

    Can you remember whether you were alone or with others—and how you felt about that afterwards?

    Can you remember how you felt physically a few hours after the shock, or the next day?

2. *Think back to a time when you were with another person who received bad news. How did that person react?*

    Was there anything you could do to help? What did you do?

If you are studying with a group

a) *Share the answers you have for questions 1 and 2 and learn from the experience of others.*

b) *Discuss if there is anything your group can do to arrange to be with people who might need company after they have been given bad news.*

CHAPTER EIGHT

The struggle for control

Janice's reaction to the news of her husband's fatal accident was violent and hysterical. Her doctor gave her an injection and she slept for a while. She was disoriented when she woke and still refused to accept the fact of her husband's death. She drifted back to sleep again.

Hours later, when the injection was beginning to wear off, Janice began to acknowledge that something was wrong. She became aware that she was in bed, in daylight, with her neighbour hovering around, full of concern. She began to remember the words she had been told, and she wept quietly.

Mrs Smith reached out to comfort her, and between her sobs, Janice began to say, 'I'm sorry . . . must be keeping you back . . . sorry . . . can't help it.' She was coming out of shock, and a struggle was going on in her mind:

> *'What are you doing in bed at four o'clock in the afternoon, carrying on like this? Mrs Smith is having to look after you! You must be wasting her time! Get a grip on yourself!'*
>
> *'I can't . . . Drew's dead . . . I'm crying again . . .'*
>
> *'What'll Mrs Smith think of you, weeping like this in front of her? Come on now, Janice!'*
>
> *'I'll try . . . I'll apologise.'*

Cultural norms influence behaviour at the Control Stage

Janice is British and, firmly lodged within her, are all the accepted norms of British culture. Within that society, Janice belongs to some sub-cultures. She is white, female, and middle-class. She lives in a city suburb, far from her original home. She attends the local Methodist Church. Janice was brought up in a family who helped others—not in one which received help. All this, and more besides, will condition how Janice feels she ought to behave—even in the midst of tragedy.

In many ways, Janice's programming makes it difficult for her to express her grief, once the shock stage has passed. People of different cultures, even of different sub-cultures, have vastly different guidelines and assumptions programmed into them. This is, perhaps, the stage of grief where these are most noticeable. People do what they feel they *ought* to do.

Some cultures expect mourners to beat their breasts, pull out their hair, to scream, to wail, to tear their clothes, to dance, even to inflict wounds upon their bodies. They do so because these are normal practices to them. I expect that societies like these have fewer problems than we do with unexpressed grief!

This stage in the grief process can be named the 'Control Stage'. It is not given this name because people in this stage of grief appear to be in control of their emotions, but because, at this stage, cultural expectations and practices largely control the way in which a mourner is free to express grief.

Culture or Christianity?

By and large, British society encourages emotional self-control for women and expects it from men. Often this suppression of feeling is reinforced by church teaching and can cause people needless, drawn-out suffering to add to their grief. Have you overheard this kind of conversation? 'Of course, she was very brave. She kept up for the sake of the children.' Or 'What a witness! They were comforting others at their own son's funeral! There was only one part when I thought he was not going to pull through, and that was when they sang . . .'

These examples illustrate the expectations often held by kind, well-meaning people. But they are contrary to the way we have been created to function and also to what the Bible teaches.

Jesus wept when he was sad. In Romans 12 we are encouraged to 'weep with those who weep'. The widows of the early church wept when their friend Dorcas died. The Old Testament contains many references to both men and women weeping. We are taught to look forward to a day when 'God will wipe away every tear' from the eyes of those who have come through persecution, but, until that day, expressing sorrow in tears seems to be entirely natural for those he has created.

The Control Stage begins the struggle to face the loss

Janice entered the Control Stage as she focussed on the reason for Mrs Smith being with her, and as she began to worry about what she must think. And so something stirs inside the mourner with a message that life must go on. Hurting and bewildered, he or she responds by looking out at a new phase of life—one without the person or thing that has been lost.

A Sense of Unreality

The hallmark of the Control Phase is numbness. The loss has happened, but the person suffering the loss is not yet prepared to feel its full impact. There is a sense of unreality, a feeling of lightheadedness and often nausea. It feels like being in a dream-world from which it may be possible to waken to find things as they were before the loss.

It is common for someone in this condition to set a place at table for the person who has gone, or to say to themselves, 'I must remember to tell X that when he comes home,' only to remember that X will not be coming home again. It is as if the mourner has to have an occasional rest from facing the loss and so the mind is given permission for one or two lapses from harsh reality.

The span of concentration at this time is distressingly short. Just as the mind sometimes chooses to forget that the loss has occurred, so it will refuse to stay on any other subject without wandering back to the fact of the loss. A neighbour will drop in. If he talks too much—not knowing what to say—the mourner will lose the thread of the conversation. Often someone in the initial stages of grief will turn on the television set or pick up a good novel, just to escape for a while. Inevitably, the mind drifts back to mourning.

Do not go rushing round to a newly bereaved household with a wonderful book you feel sure will help them. Each time they look at it, they are more likely to feel guilty at not having got round to reading it than feel helped by its words of wisdom. Keep it till later—and even then, offer with it the option of not taking it.

Most of us seem to feel that we have to know what to say to someone recently bereaved. The fact is that most mourners will take in very little of what is said to them at this stage and will remember even less afterwards.

The Need for Touch

In an earlier chapter, I told the story of Cathy whose cat Sebastian had to be put down. Her little sister, Libby, had always given Sebastian a cuddle first thing in the morning, and last thing at night. After he was buried, Libby asked, 'What can I do now that I have no Sebastian to cuddle?' Very firmly her big sister stated, 'We don't want to have another cat!' 'But,' Libby replied, 'I don't mean for having, I just mean for holding!'

What does reach a person in this phase is touch—warm, caring, human contact that demands nothing in return. Many long just to be held—to return for a moment or two (or perhaps much longer) to a time in infancy when bad feelings were made much better by the closeness of a loving parent who seemed to understand and to give total acceptance. Unfortunately, some people have no such memory to awaken. They may shrink back from any form of human contact and this should not be forced upon them.

People often want suggestions as to what to say to one who has just lost someone close. Words like 'I'm so sorry' or 'I'll be thinking of you', along with a handshake or a hug can be quite sufficient, unless a longer conversation is called for.

Sometimes people who would like to comfort others physically, are afraid to do so because of sexual feelings or needs which might be aroused, either in themselves, or in those they want to comfort (see story on page 27). For the majority of people in very early bereavement, that fear is groundless. The needs aroused are more like those for a parent, than for a sexual partner (though these needs may well be clamant in subsequent weeks). Physical touch at such a time can help a mourner loosen some of the need for control and to cry. It is all right to be like a little child again if a warm and protective parent is present. If, however, you are afraid that you may not be able to control your sexual feelings, it is better for you to recognise this and not to risk damaging the relationship you have with the bereaved person.

If someone allows you the privilege of holding him or her while tears express and release some of their sadness, think of yourself as a loving parent for him or her and let your responses be those you would make towards a child whom you both love and respect. Do not be afraid to hold that child till the tears have gone, and the deep sighs and the words which might be voiced. If words come, accept them, as words that need to be said. Often they need no reply save the love felt through touch (see story p. 135). To reject such words with 'Don't feel like that!' or 'Hush—not now!' or 'Don't question God's ways' can reject the person who has shared them with you. It will be much less easy for him or her to share such vulnerability again for a long time.

The Need to talk

One of the first tasks in the grief process is for the mourner to put into words the brutal facts of the loss.

Harold was called to the managing director's office one morning along with other colleagues. They were bluntly told they would be made redundant in two months' time. He couldn't believe it. Normally he shared with his wife everything that affected them as a couple, but when he got home that evening, he did not mention it to her. Eventually he did tell her, succumbing to the sheer pressure of the knowledge that she would find out through someone else sooner or later if he did not.

It was only when he put it into words for Helen, that he began, realistically, to face up to his redundancy. While he had kept it to himself, he could pretend that another job would turn up. It was even more painful than he had thought it might be. Hearing the word 'Redundant!' echoed from Helen's lips when he told her meant that he could no longer run from the fact.

Have you ever noticed how adults will tell over and over again, the blow-by-blow details of how an accident happened or of what took place from the time a pain began, till death occurred? The story will be repeated to all who visit and to all who phone. This constant repetition, with its minute attention to detail, may seem macabre or as likely to bring about an unnecessary re-opening of wounds to those who listen to the story from the sidelines. If you are in the position of being one who listens, learn to accept any discomfort you may feel about the repetition. By telling and then retelling the story, the one in the situation of loss is gradually convincing herself that it has all actually happened to her and to someone close to her. The retelling of it seems to be therapeutic. This will stop when it is no longer necessary.

Do not shield the bereaved from phone calls or visitors, nor from answering letters, unless it is obvious to you that it is no longer helping them to express their grief. Only take over if you are sure that these activities are draining them of the resources of energy they need to cope with all they have to do or of time to sleep or to be alone, in touch with their loss.

It is helpful to talk about how the loss happened, and it is good to talk about the person who has died or about the particular loss involved. Encourage the bereaved to recall happy or significant times and to put their memories into words. One minister I know, on his first visit to a bereaved spouse, makes a habit of asking, 'And how did you two meet in the first place?' Remembering good experiences, and listening to those others share from their memories, can help those in loss feel treasured and significant.

The First Times

During the Control Stage of the grief process, the bereaved person begins to face doing all the things they used to do but, for the first time, doing these without the one they have lost. Usually, the longer each of these 'first times' is delayed, the harder it is to face. The sooner they are faced, the easier it is for life to go on and for adjustment to occur.

Some people go to great lengths to attempt to shield others from pain. I heard of one persistent woman who wanted to climb into bed beside her widowed neighbour on the day her husband died, because she couldn't bear to think of her sleeping alone! Hard though it is for most to face the empty double bed, it is usually best for the person to sleep alone as soon as possible, even if sleep does not come. The grief process is painful. To avoid the pain, is also to avoid the healing which springs from it.

The recently bereaved often wonder, on the first time they meet a friend or neighbour after the death, if that person had heard about their loss. Do not delay in saying that you do know, even if you find it awkward to make the first approach. Many avoid the bereaved or the recently divorced or those made redundant, because they feel they do not know what to say. This isolation from normal social contact can make readjustment even more difficult than it need be. Widows or widowers can appreciate the offer by a friend to accompany them on the first time they go to church or to a club or even out shopping. 'First times', although they begin from the time of the loss, go on for at least a year. There will be the first birthday, the first holiday, the first Christmas and New Year, each bringing back its own memories. Those who have lost a parent, even if they have grown up and left home, often find it hard on the first occasion when they fall ill or the first time they feel they need advice or the first time they have some success or achievement which would have given them particular satisfaction. Sometimes a visit, a phone call, or even a note from a friend can be so much appreciated as a form of support at an appropriate 'first' occasion.

Letters

If you look down the column of death notices in any newspaper, you will almost certainly find some which say 'No letters please.' Receiving letters of sympathy can be extremely painful, and I can understand why some people try to avoid this—and also the chore of replying to each one. But during the Control Stage of grief, letters come in, bidden or not.

Many bereaved people have found tremendous comfort and support from the letters they have received—even those who felt at the time that they did not want them. Just because it can be well nigh impossible to deal with the rush of letters which can arrive around the time of the funeral, those to whom they are sent often find themselves re-reading them weeks later, in order to answer them. I believe that good letters can be very supportive indeed just around that time when the first rush of concerned support is fading.

Lots of people feel moved to write letters, but find it extremely difficult to know what to say. Here are a few guidelines which might help:

If you knew the person who has died then say something about what he or she meant to you. If you have a special memory of that person that you treasure and that you think it would be good to share, then share it.

Do not assume that you know how the person to whom you are writing will feel, or what he or she is thinking! If you can, share how you feel about the loss.

If there is something you can genuinely offer by way of support, then offer it.

Keep your letter short and to the point. Don't use the occasion to preach at the bereaved!

Letters which feel insincere can be very hurtful. Letters which say something positive can be treasured and used over and over again as the mourner feels the need to be reassured that the person who was so important to him or her, was valued by others too.

Physical Reactions

At the Control Stage of grief the body will be reacting from the shock experienced. It is very common for people to feel extremely tired, mentally and physically, yet to be unable to sleep soundly. If sleep does come, it is sometimes accompanied by vivid dreams. For some, the dreams will be of the lost person happy and well; for others there might be terrifying nightmares, reliving the loss. Generally, the whole digestive system of a mourner will be upset. Here again, opposites can happen. Either the persons concerned will have little interest in food or will begin to eat, drink or smoke compulsively. Either constipation or diarrhoea are likely. Some feel continuously nauseous, and flatulence is common. Sometimes an itchy rash develops in some areas of the body.

These physical reactions, and others, are common. Some quickly disappear as the mourner recovers from the initial shock. Others may persist into the next stage of the grief process.

Medical Help

When there has been a death in the family, the family doctor will often take care of the bereaved. A sedative may be prescribed to help them sleep and perhaps a tranquilliser to help them cope with the physical and psychological reactions to their grief. Unfortunately, these drugs can be addictive, and in later weeks and months, the grieving person may find it very difficult to stop them, with resulting long-term dependency and side effects. Also, tranquillisers may retard the grief process by inappropriately cushioning the pain of bereavement and delaying the person's ability to face up to life again.

Due to time and demands on their service, some doctors find it easier and quicker to give and repeat a prescription rather than to listen and give counselling help. Many doctors, however, are now aware of the disadvantages of such drugs, and will prescribe them only if they feel the grieving person would be unable to cope without them. Many people in our society today are taking some form of tranquiliser. Some may offer their own pills to a grieving person if the doctor has not prescribed any. This could be dangerous, *and* bad for the bereaved. Discourage it!

Practical Arrangements after a Death

During the Control Stage of mourning after a death in the family, many practical arrangements have to be attended to. Most of these cannot wait until the bereaved feel better or more like attending to them! Often help and support are appreciated here. It is very common nowadays for an adult to be middle-aged before he or she experiences a death in the family. Most people do not know what has to be done in such a situation because they have not encountered it before. Fortunately for the rest of us, there are those whose professions bring them face to face with this on a regular basis—doctors, the clergy, undertakers. Most of these are more than willing to give guidance to those who need it.

If you are in the position of encountering this situation as a helper, but are still unsure of all that has to be done, there is an extremely practical and useful publication available from Citizens' Advice Bureaux, entitled 'In the Event of Death . . .' This is a Scottish publication and it deals specifically with legal matters surrounding death in Scotland.* It is written by David Nichols in language for lay persons.

Age Concern has recently brought out a very helpful four-page form. In it, there is space to record information on where to contact a person's next-of-kin, doctor, minister, lawyer, and so on. Details about bank accounts, insurance policies, and the will are set out, so that all the necessary information is immediately accessible for anyone who has to deal with the practical details of that person's death. If such a form is filled out before the death and then kept where it will be easily found, it can save a lot of time and effort for those involved. If you are in regular contact with any elderly persons or with others who live alone, it might be good to recommend this document to them.

An Exercise

For you to think through by yourself, or to share with others

1. *If you have ever been through a time of close bereavement, what do you remember bringing comfort to you?*
   Do you remember anything done by a well-meaning person which you found hurtful or unhelpful?
2. *Can you remember any time in your life when a loss left you wanting physical contact from others? If so, did you have your needs met?*

---

*This, unfortunately, does not apply to England, Wales, or N. Ireland, where the legal situation is different.

3. *If you have ever had an experience of bereavement, did any particular passage or a text from Scripture have special significance to you in it? If you did, can you think why these words were significant to you then?*

   Do you think these would be significant for every grieving person or would the significance depend on something beyond the actual words?

4. *How comfortable would you feel about holding a grieving person closely while he or she wept, if that person was*
   a) *a person of similar age and the same sex as yourself?*
   b) *a person of similar age but of the opposite sex?*
   c) *a younger person than you?*
   d) *a much older person than you?*

5. *Are there some kinds of help best given in a time of grief by close friends and relatives? If so, which, and why?*

   Are there some kinds of help best given by neighbours or colleagues? If so, which and why?

   Are there some best given by professional care-agents, such as ministers, doctors, health visitors, and social workers? If so, which and why?

CHAPTER NINE

Each grieving is unique

An Exercise

For you to think through by yourself, or with a small group

> *In your life so far, have you had two losses of the same kind*
> *eg have you left two jobs?*
> > *have you twice been in hospital?*
> > *have you suffered two close bereavements?*
>
> *If so, did you have exactly the same reactions on each*
> *occasion, or were your experiences different from one*
> *another?*

It is likely that from answering these questions that you will
have discovered that each loss you have suffered has been
unique in some way. If that is so within one personality it
certainly is true where more than one person is involved. Each
one grieves uniquely.

Two Widows in one Parish

In a parish where I worked some years ago, two women who
lived in adjoining streets were widowed within the same week.
One of these women had a young family and a job and was
back at work a few days after her husband's funeral. The
other had a grown-up family and was not employed. She stayed
in her house and her many friends visited her, went shopping
for her and wept with her.

A few weeks after their bereavements, the widows met by

chance in the street. 'It's very obvious to me,' the older widow said to the younger one, 'that you can't have loved your husband as much as I did, or you couldn't be going around now as if nothing had happened.' The older widow was assuming that the only right way for a loving wife to mourn the death of her husband was in the way that she was grieving for hers.

People in grief are so vulnerable, and so often preoccupied with their own way of expressing grief that there seems to be little room in some families for mutual understanding and for allowing people to do what they feel they need to do to keep themselves safe.

Parents of the same Child

Rachel and Duncan were loving parents to two happy and healthy little daughters. Then Rachel gave birth to a son and their family seemed complete. Four months later, Rachel found the baby lying lifeless in his pram when she went to lift him from his afternoon nap. Their doctor could give no explanation as to why a perfectly healthy child should have what is known as a 'cot death'.

Duncan's reaction to the death of their infant son was to throw himself into his work and to be away from home even more than usual. When he was home at weekends he seemed almost to be avoiding the other two children. When he did play with them, it was without the energy and spirit he had always shown before his beareavement.

Rachel's pattern of coping was in complete contrast to Duncan's. She began to cling, both physically and emotionally, to her two surviving children. She was rarely away from her home and seemed afraid to let them go out of her sight. She saw Duncan's absence as a rejection both of her and of their daughters, just at the very time when she yearned to have the reassurance of his physical presence in the house, his arms around her to calm the guilt and fright she felt so strongly. But she could not tell him how she felt because she was sure he no longer cared. She blamed him for not realising what she needed and at least trying to meet her needs. Finally she became convinced that he was deliberately acting in this way to punish her for letting his son die.

Duncan was not, in fact, trying to punish Rachel. He was trying to keep himself together—not to go to pieces. The only way he knew to do that was to try not to think about it, so he plunged into work and kept away from all the visible reminders of his pain. He had been overjoyed at the birth of his son. He loved both his daughters dearly, but somehow, the arrival of his son had affirmed his manhood in a special way. His world which had seemed so secure and complete and right had been shattered without any warning. Not realising what he was doing, he had begun to cushion himself against any more unbearable blows by putting more emotional distance between him and the others he loved. When Rachel and the girls reached out to him, he could not risk responding as he had in the past in case they were taken from him too. It was easier for him not to see them.

Friends and relatives who were aware of what was going on in that family did not know what to do about it. They began to take sides, and the split between Rachel and Duncan grew wider as it was reinforced.

Eventually, they divorced.

Helping different Members of the same Family

It can be very awkward to visit in the home of a grieving family where each seems to need a different kind of support. What helps one may not help the others. One might need to talk: the other might want silence and simply to be held.

In John's Gospel there is a story of Jesus visiting two sisters who had recently lost their brother. One wanted to talk with Jesus about her brother's resurrection, and the other was so emotionally upset, she could hardly talk at all. Strangely enough, it seems as if they both said almost identical words as Jesus met them, but his way of responding to them was to meet the *unique* need of each individual.

Many people who wish to be a comfort and support to grieving people want to be told what to reply if a mourner asks a particular question. 'What will I say to him if he says, "How can a loving God allow this to happen?"' someone might ask. There is no easy answer to that question. The answer depends on the needs of the grieving individual and the sensitivity and understanding of the one giving support. But look for yourself at the story of how Jesus responded.

An Exercise

For you to think through by yourself, or with a small group.

1. *Look up the Gospel of St John, chapter 11, and read it right through.*

2. *Verses 20 to 28, and then verse 39 show Martha's way of coping with her grief four days after her bereavement.*

   Verse 20, and then verses 28 to 33 show Mary's way of coping.

   Note what each sister did and said. Contrast one with the other.

3. *Now look at the words they both used—'If you had been here, Lord, my brother would not have died.' (v. 21, and v. 32)*

   From your reading of the story, what tone of voice do you imagine Martha used and what tone might Mary have said them in?

   Do you imagine the sisters had exactly the same feelings as they said these same words?

   Look to see whether or not Jesus responded to each in the same way.

   What can you learn from the way he responded in each situation?

Loving Attention

Each individual within a family, requires loving attention
and help after a severe loss. And what is true for adults, is
most certainly true for children. (See chapter 10.) It may be
that each member of the family needs support from a different
friend or care-agent, but the emphasis nowadays is moving
towards helping different members of the family to get back
into communication with each other after a bereavement. Most
families have resources to support any one member during a
time of crisis. This support system needs to be given help to
become a mutual one where each understands the other if all
are grieving at the same time.

Years ago, I sat in a circle on the floor of a log cabin. In the
centre, on cushions, sat a young couple, facing each other. We
were all part of a House Church group on a weekend away
together. That couple were still living together, but, since they
had experienced the death of one of their children, communication had been strained between them.

It was one of the most moving experiences I can remember.
The leader helped them to begin to tell each other what the
death of their baby had meant to them: what they had felt,
and how they coped with their grief. The misunderstandings
and blamings nursed for years were cleared up in one short
hour during which they had loving supportive friends around
them. The young couple wept and the whole group wept with
them. They embraced and we all embraced them.

In Britain there is an increasing expertise in the area of
family therapy. Many social workers and other care-agents are
receiving training in working with families as a whole, rather
than in dealing with individuals. Tragedies do bring some
people closer to each other, but it seems as if they are also at
least as likely to split couples and force families apart. If you
have the opportunity of being involved with a family in grief,
help the members to begin to talk openly in front of each
other about their thoughts, feelings, fears, and their ways of

coping with their loss. As individual members begin to understand not only their own behaviour under stress but also that
of the other members, new possibilities of growing together
open up. As they understand more, they can accept and forgive
more and learn how to support one another and handle the
reality of their loss more creatively.

An Exercise

For you to think through by yourself, or with others.

1. *Have you ever experienced a grief situation where relationships were strained for a time with the others involved?
   If so, what happened to help you come together again?*
2. *If you had been a friend of Rachel and Duncan at the time
   of the death of their baby son, what might you have tried to
   do to help them begin to understand each other better before
   they decided to split up?*

CHAPTER TEN

Grieving children

In our culture it is still comparatively common to attempt to shield children from the experience of grief. I have talked with scores of adults who remember, still with some fear and bewilderment, an early experience of death within their family circle. These long-held emotions do not normally stem from being present at the death, but from the way the adults around them at the time reacted to it. Many remember being whisked off to the home of a relative or neighbour and being brought back again, only to discover that one of the family was no longer there. Some have no recollection of being told what had happened. Others remember being told something they did not fully understand. They knew, however, from the way people acted that they were not supposed to ask questions about it. Some were warned not to talk about what had happened in case it would upset mother or granny.

Those who have lived with terminally ill parents or grandparents over a period of months or even years of their childhood, sometimes still carry guilt from the time the death occurred. They have memories of having to be quiet and good in case they made the sick person worse. How were they to know, if no-one reassured them, that it was not their noise or badness that did kill them? Their fertile imaginations had usually worked over-time, frightening and confusing them. Many had picked up weird gossip from playmates. Surprisingly few adults, as they have grown-up, have asked their parents to clear up for them the stories of what actually happened during those events from childhood years. Have you done so?

When an adult is in a state of shock it is not possible for him or her to sit down with a child to explain what has happened. But most people come out of shock quickly and are able to tell others—even their children. They may not be able to share the news without expressing a great deal of emotion, but this is healthy both for the adult to express and for the children to see. Children go into shock just as adults do, but usually the Control Stage of grief is not so obvious in children. With most children, the sense of loss completely overwhelms any need to meet expectations in others. They are more likely to express their grief quite openly and spontaneously.

Jonathan

Jonathan was thirteen years old but was, in many ways, immature for his years. He had been born physically handicapped and had been over-protected throughout a sheltered upbringing in a close family. He was especially close to his mother. His father had difficulty in accepting the fact that his son had been born handicapped.

Jonathan was being educated at a residential school when the staff received a phone call asking them to tell him that his mother had died very suddenly and that his father was on his way to see him. His housekeeper took him off to a room where they could be alone together while she told him. Normally he was a very quiet, withdrawn lad. Immediately on hearing the news he went into a violent rage, throwing himself around the room, stamping and yelling. When he had exhausted himself, he appeared to be quite confused for a while as if he could not remember what had happened and why he was behaving as he was. He then went to his housemother and stretched his hand out to her. While she held it, he sobbed inconsolably.

After his tears stopped, Jonathan followed his housemother around the building as she went on with her work, until his father arrived. The staff left father and son alone together.

As soon as his father left the school, Jonathan headed for

his transistor radio, put on his headphones, and withdrew completely from the world of the residential school. He would not come for supper. He was looking after himself. He had taken enough pain for a time. So he surrounded himself with the reassurance and comfort of the familiar sounds of pop music. That had not changed.

Mandy

Mandy had been born at the end of a large family and was a Down's Syndrome baby. As the rest of the family grew up and left home, Mandy stayed behind with her mother. She was in her twenties when her mother died. The family told Mandy what had happened and took her to her mother's funeral, but it was very difficult for Mandy to understand the implications of what she had been told.

At the family gathering for the funeral her brothers and sisters sat around formally with their spouses, waiting for the minister to conduct the service. Mandy did not know what to make of what was going on, so she decided to use this time to help herself make sense of it all. She rose from her seat and went to the person next to her. 'Knock. Knock,' she said. In the embarrassed silence, he replied to her, 'Who's there?' 'Mummy!' she said firmly. 'Ssh! Go and sit down, Mandy!' he whispered.

But Mandy did not want to sit down. Round the circle she went, inviting responses to her repeated, 'Knock. Knock.' The family were obviously at a loss to know how to react and most embarrassed in front of the minister whom they did not know. Mandy was undeterred. On she went till she came to where the minister was sitting, and 'Knock. Knock,' she challenged him. 'Who's there, Mandy?' he asked. 'Mummy!' came the answer again. Going along with the pattern she seemed to want, the minister responded, 'Mummy who?' 'Mummy's dead!' said Mandy. 'That's right, Mandy. Mummy's dead,' he said to her gently, taking her on his knee and holding her there while he gave the rest of the family the necessary instructions before the service.

Mandy had known what she needed to do to look after herself. The minister confessed afterwards to feeling very awkward and very much at a loss to know what he ought to do, sensing the family's embarrassment. By the time Mandy had reached him, he had made the decision to focus on her need since it seemed to be clamant. He guessed what Mandy's mother might have done with the bewildered little girl in the body of the grown woman in front of him. He took her on his knee and held her as he would have done spontaneously, had she been three or four years of age.

Tina

For four years, Tina and her sister Lisa had been in a local authority children's home. Lisa was fourteen and did not want to be adopted. Tina wanted to be part of a new family but wished Lisa would want the same. An adoptive family was found for Tina some distance from the home. Even before she went to live with them, Tina had informed her new family that she wanted no cuddles or kisses from them.

After a few days with her new parents, Tina had to have a day off her new school. She felt dizzy and very tired. A day in her warm bed with her new mother thinking up every possible thing to make her feel better seemed to set her on her feet again. Then Tina began to feel itchy all over—even on the soles of her feet! There was no sign of a rash. Again the new mother fussed over her—this time with soothing lotion for her itch.

'Why am I all itchy?' Tina asked her as she smoothed on the lotion. 'I'm not sure. I can't see any spots, but would you like to know what I think it may be?' 'What?' Tina asked. 'Sometimes when people lose someone very special to them, they get very itchy,' the mother offered. Immediately Tina said, 'Lisa!'

Later on that evening, the mother overheard Tina explaining

this situation to Lisa on the phone. After Tina had gone to bed, she found written on the telephone pad.

> *Hello Lisa. Are you itchy? I am.*
> *Signed Tina.*
> *XXX*

The itch had disappeared by the time the girls saw each other, three days later.

It seemed as if Tina's body needed the reassurance that comes from touch although Tina's independent spirit would not allow it as a sign of premature intimacy in the new relationship. She could give herself permission to get extra attention through being tired and itchy but not, just yet, through being loved.

If adults around grieving children are able to respond sensitively, the children will look after themselves, by, in one way or another, expressing their needs.

Neglect of Children in Grief

The danger with grieving children is that their needs will be overlooked and that they will be left very much on their own, to come to terms with their mourning as best they can. Parents normally attend to the needs of their children. If these mothers or fathers are in the initial stages of grief, then they themselves, are needing help from others. If they are too needy, they have no resources adequate to look after their children's emotional needs.

Callum

Callum was only five years of age when his parents' relationship began to deteriorate. As often as not, his father would come home very late at night and Callum would be wakened by his parents fighting. The first time that happened he had felt very frightened. Earlier that evening he had been naughty while his mother was having a long conversation with his granny on the phone. He was bored and wanted her to play with him. He knew she had seen him poking his pencil through the seat of the chair but she pretended she hadn't. So he did it again. His mother had stopped talking to granny just long enough to shout at him, 'Just you wait until your daddy comes home!' and then had gone on with her long phone call. Now his father was home and he sounded very angry. Callum put his head under his bedclothes to hide but his father didn't come to punish him.

Each time Callum heard his parents fighting he thought it must be something to do with him. Since he was a normal five-year-old, he rarely got through a whole day without some minor incident his mother did not appreciate. Sometimes, after he should have been asleep, he would hear his mother sobbing by herself in the bedroom next door. One evening he tried to go to be with her, to comfort her. At first she had not heard him as he stood there. When she did see him, she had snapped, 'Go to bed!' He had asked her if she had a sore tummy. She had said 'No.' Then he had asked her if she had a sore head. She had said, 'Callum, please go back to bed and go to sleep.' But Callum stood there, desperately wanting his mother to stop crying and not knowing what to do to help her. 'Where's Daddy?' he said, thinking he might know what to do to help her. His mother stopped crying, got off her bed, carried him roughly to his room, flung him on top of his bed, and spanked him. 'Now, stay there!' she yelled at him and left him alone.

Throughout all this, Callum's mother kept her son fed and clothed, but she hardly ever played with him. She never tried to explain to Callum why she was so sad and short-tempered nor why his father was so rarely there for him. Callum had to come to his own conclusions and to look after his own feelings as best he could. Fortunately, he had a warm and perceptive school-teacher who sensed that something must be wrong at home. Eventually, she talked to the head teacher who sent for his mother. By that time, his father had left home.

Callum was given help from the Child Guidance Services available through the school. With some assistance from the educational psychologist, Callum's mother was able to talk to him about what had been happening around him at home. She had no idea that he might have felt to blame for it all. But the main reason for doing nothing about Callum was that she was caught up in her pain and loneliness. The man who had loved her had found someone more lovable and she felt rejected, ugly and useless.

What can be done to help?

Any help and support that is given to grieving parents, and which meets some of their needs, is likely to lessen the burden that can fall on children who feel they have to try to do this. Many people who suffered a family bereavement in childhood will tell a story of how they felt that from that point on, they had to take on adult responsibilities and leave their childhood behind. The loss of a parent of either sex will often cause a growing child of that same sex to feel that he or she has now to fill that place in the family. This is especially true with eldest daughters on the death of their mother and eldest sons at the loss of their father.

But equally, there can be a swing in the opposite direction. Sometimes parents can be so aware of the grief in their children and of their role in helping them through that grief, that they can neglect their own personal mourning. This is not a healthy thing for the adults concerned and may lead to delayed complications in what could have been a natural process for them. Nor is it good for the children. A father who fought bravely not to cry in front of his children after the sudden death of their mother was told afterwards that they had come to the conclusion between themselves that he had not loved her much since he showed no signs of mourning! Parents who are able to weep with their children are giving them a healthy permission to express sadness in an appropriate way.

Any help that can be given to families to restore communication after a major loss will be of great value to all. Although some people in intense situations of grief may benefit from professional help for a time, most of the normal adjustment back to a meaningful life after a loss is facilitated by caring people who live and work alongside those who mourn. Children need to talk about the person they have lost. If their parents, or remaining parent, find this very difficult to share with them, then they need other adults to talk with adults who are around and available for them to talk to when they feel like it. And this kind of support should ideally go on for some time and not happen only at the time of the loss. And, just as much as adults do, children can need others to help them express some of their very deep feelings. Children can store up anger until it becomes depression or until it comes out in anti-social behaviour. Children will live with unnecessary guilt for years after a bereavement or some other breakdown in family relationships. Just like adults in grief, children feel helpless, and unable to cope with all that is going on inside themselves.

If a child has suffered the loss of a brother or sister, there may be an even greater need for help outside the family. It is all too easy for the remaining children to begin to feel that they can never measure up to the one who has been taken, and for parents unwittingly to idolise the dead child and neglect the living. Sometimes it needs a very brave and loving outsider to confront this kind of unconscious behaviour and to re-unite the parents with the children who need them.

An Exercise

For you to think through by yourself or with a small group

  1. Are you in regular contact with children at work, in your family or neighbourhood, or through organisations?
    If so, are you aware of any of them who might be in a loss situation at the moment? Can you think of any way in

which you might be able to help them grow through this loss?

2. *If you are studying this book with a small group from a specific organisation, do you have the opportunity to work with children or to work with families, or do you aim only to support adults?*

   Is there anything your group could do for children or for families from your reading of this chapter?

CHAPTER ELEVEN

Our need for ritual

For the high points, and for the crises in life, humankind has invented rituals. Birth, puberty or coming-of-age, marriage, dying, death and mourning—all of these are events in which the individual is caught up in something larger and more meaningful than what is happening there and then. Long established rituals reflect the accumulated wisdom of generations, handed down through those who are its guardians in each culture. Individual lives, significant or insignificant as others might see them, are thus given permission to grow and develop, to move on safely through change to the next agreed stage of their journey in life within their society.

Ritual practices have tended to move away from the family and the community into the hands of people who are professionally involved with those who die and with those who mourn them. Doctors, undertakers and the clergy now know and perpetuate the rituals that remain. There are, however, some areas scattered throughout rural and island Britain where traditional ritual has remained strong and supportive.

In the Outer Hebrides it is still the practice when a person dies that the whole adult population of the community will gather at the bereaved home each evening between the death and the funeral to pray, sing psalms, read the Bible and listen to the preaching of a minister or lay preacher. Every adult male will be expected to attend the funeral and all work will cease in the village to let this happen.

In many of the fishing villages along the east coast of Scotland, a bereavement in the family gives the signal for the women of the community to bake and cook. The kitchen door of the home where the death has occurred is left unlocked and neighbours come in to lay food on the kitchen table for the grieving family and for the meal after the funeral, to which the whole community will come.

After that meal, all leave except those closest to the family who then sit round the fire, talking. Their talk is of the character of the person who has died. Together they recall incidents in which they were involved with the deceased. This mourning ritual is also carried out in the homes of those fishermen lost at sea, although there sometimes can be no burial service because the bodies have not been recovered.

Friends and far-flung family members still gather around to be present at a funeral or memorial service for those who die in urban communities, but the rituals which used to give structure to the time before the funeral have largely passed away in city life.

Many who feel they ought to call at the grieving home in the days before the funeral do not know what to do when they call, because there is no longer any accepted pattern laid down. In very recent years, it was still the practice, even in cities, for the body to lie in its open coffin so that friends, neighbours and even young children, could pay their last respects to the dead by coming to say goodbye. Many would kiss the face of the corpse or leave a few flowers in the coffin. They would pray beside it or talk to the body that had housed the spirit of the one they had known and loved. Nowadays this practice comes into our homes from other cultures through the news on our television screens. We watch as the body of Mrs Gandhi is borne to her funeral pyre or the great leaders of Russia lie in state while thousands file past to pay homage. But in our homes now, the body is generally removed in its coffin to a funeral parlour and the focus of attention has fallen on the bereaved.

The sole remaining ritual to mark the passage of life into death and beyond seems to be the funeral service.

An Exercise

For you to think through for yourself, or with other people.

Why should we still have funerals?

   Take a pen and paper and make a list of as many reasons as you can think of, why, in our modern country, we should still have this one remaining widely accepted ritual.

   (NB The answer 'to dispose of the body', is not sufficient because this could be done without a ritual accompanying the act.)

Why have a Funeral?

Here are many things you might have included in your list. There may also be one or two you did not consider and which you might like to think over now.

1. *For the main mourners, a funeral brings together friends and relatives for support.*
2. *It brings the main mourners the reassurance that the one they have lost was significant to others also.*
3. *A funeral is a public statement that the person being buried is dead. This marks, for all to see, the point of no return. The reality of the death can be faced.*
4. *If the funeral service uses words familiar to those who mourn, these can bring comfort and strength into the chaos of jumbled feelings which can be in the hearts of those most affected.*
5. *The funeral publicly confers a new status on those relatives who remain. (eg widow, fatherless, orphan, single parent, childless.)*
6. *For some people, the funeral will be a significant time in the process of 'saying goodbye' to the deceased person. From this point on, it will be easier for them to believe that the bodily presence of that person is no longer with them.*
7. *Many at the funeral may be feeling guilty about things said or not said, done or left undone, in their relationship*

with the deceased. If, at the service, there is a prayer of confession, this can be helpful for them. (*Remember that The Lord's Prayer includes asking for forgiveness.*)

8. In marking the end of a person's earthly life there can come to the mourners a fresh sense of their own mortality.

9. It can be a time of thanksgiving and praise for a life well-lived and 'full of days' and from which others have benefited in love, joy and wisdom.

10. It can be a time when people of various religions which believe in life beyond death celebrate the beginning of a new life for their loved ones.

11. It can be a time when those who have not thought about life after death having any reality for them or those dear to them, begin to think about this.

12. It can be a time when some of the mourners sense the presence of the deceased friend of relative in a special way.

Have you any more to add?

The Need for Proof of the Loss

It seems as if we have to *feel* that a loss has taken place. It is not enough proof for us to be given information that the loss has occurred. There is often a very emotional response within the bereaved as they watch the coffin disappear during a crematorium service. Sometimes mourners will cry out to the person they have lost or begin to weep uncontrollably. Just because this can be so distressing, some people in charge of funeral arrangements try to avoid this by arranging that the coffin sinks during a prayer or that gentle velvet curtains move silently across to hide the coffin before it is lowered. Although it may be more harrowing at that moment, it is not a cruel practice for mourners to see the coffin sink. It provides them with visible proof that they will never again see that mortal body.

When, because of illness, geographical separation or for any other reason, a person cannot attend the funeral of someone close to him or her, he or she will often have more difficulty adjusting to their loss than if proof of the death has been seen. If you can be in contact with a friend or relative who cannot have any first-hand evidence of a death having taken place, make a point of sending to that person some tangible proof that it has happened. The notice of the death in the local paper, a photograph of the gravestone, an article which belonged to the deceased—things like that can be better 'proof' of the death than that of receiving such news by letter or phone. It is completely appropriate to send such tangible evidence whenever it becomes available although it might arrive some weeks after the original notification of the death.

Those whose loved ones are 'missing, presumed dead' in war or at sea or in some accident or disaster overseas, can often refuse to believe that the death has actually taken place. Stories are common of parents, wives or sweethearts who still wait, years after everyone else has given up hope, for their missing ones to come home to them. The relatives of the British servicemen who were killed in the South Atlantic in 1982, were taken to the Falklands one year later. A journalist covering the visit reported that the widow of Captain Chris Dent said, 'It was desperately hard, very much more difficult than I expected. But it was at the moment that I knelt on the grass at Chris's grave that I realised finally that he was not waiting for me in the physical sense.'*

An Exercise

> *For you to think through by yourself, or with others*
> 1. *Do you have, in your church or community, any rituals which have helped you cope with mourning?*
>   *If you are part of a small group, you might like to share these with each other.*
> 2. *How might you help parents who ask you if you think it wise for their children of seven, ten and thirteen to attend their grandfather's funeral?*

* *Daily Mail*, Monday April 11, 1983.

CHAPTER TWELVE

Creating ritual

A funeral may be the only surviving ritual with which many mourners in the Western world of today mark the death of their loved ones.

'Christian' burial?

It is not legally necessary for a British citizen to have a minister of religion officiate at any funeral. Many automatically ask for the services of the clergy, perhaps because they have not thought through any alternative to this. And of course, many of those to be buried have had no personal faith in Christ.

Many of the clergy find themselves called upon to bury people they have never seen and to talk about them in a way that is comforting and supportive for those who mourn them! They repeat the words of a Christian burial service over those who have had nothing to do with the church while alive and in the presence of relatives and friends to whom the words of the service may mean very little.

Are there Alternatives?

Most denominations nowadays provide their clergy with alternative funeral services from which they can choose the one most appropriate for use in particular circumstances.

A few people are beginning to be much more creative, especially with memorial services, where there is more time for preparation. Some of these are designed to give a high degree of participation by all or some of those present. This in itself can greatly help the mourning process as people are caught up in the drama of saying goodbye.

Internal Ceremony

I have before me the duplicated programme of one fascinating service, held two months after a very gifted man had been lost at sea from his yacht. It was held on an evening in London and was a two-part programme with an interval between. Friends were invited to attend either part or both. The first hour and a half was designated 'Valediction'. The emphasis was on the celebration of the joy of living expressed through the many interests in which the man had shared while alive. Several of his friends were invited to speak informally, one about each of these interests and of the deceased's special contribution to them. Interspersed with the speeches, his favourite music was played. Friends coming had been invited to bring with them a candle. Those who had done so were encouraged to light theirs from a large central candle during the interval, and then to place it nearby. This 'interval ceremony' was meant to be a private ritual where each individual put his or her own meaning into the act, in preparation for the communal one to follow.

The second part of the evening was called 'The Mourning Ceremony'. This began with the screening of a recording from a TV series in which the person mourned had featured, talking about his chief interest. The ceremony following that, was derived from two ancient rituals; one was from the Maori people while the other was North American Indian in origin. During the mourning ceremony, any who wished to do so were encouraged to come forward and address directly the friend they had met to remember. Those who preferred to put into writing privately what they wanted to say to him were encouraged to write it on a piece of paper and then place that in a bowl at the front of the gathering. The ritual concluded with the candles being extinguished, one by one, and the papers in the bowl being burned in silence, like an offering. In the darkness the words were recited of an ancient Indian Night Chant.

The record of that most creative ritual moves me. I was not present at that ceremony but to have been there must have been a very meaningful way of saying goodbye to a loved and honoured friend. Could we who are Christians begin to create such rich rituals, weaving the ancient traditions into positive ceremonies for today's living—to shout 'Alleluia—and thanks!' for those who have gone ahead?

Small Group Ritual

Many Christian lay folk are now in various types of house group fellowships. Those groups which lay stress on deepening the quality of their loving and caring for each other feel the loss of a member deeply. If that member leaves because he or she is moving geographically too far away to continue to attend, could not the house group create a meaningful farewell ceremony instead of merely the presentation of a book with all the signatures on the flyleaf?

If a member dies, one way to cope with mourning in such a group is to have some kind of memorial service in the group with everyone taking part. It is very helpful for mourning if that can include an informal way of 'saying goodbye'. Some Christians feel unhappy at the thought of addressing that member as if he or she were still there in spirit, although others find this meaningful while the memory of their bodily presence is still very fresh in the group. To share that is not to take part in a seance! A more acceptable way for most is to have a time of prayer in which each person gives thanks for a particular quality seen in the member being remembered or a particular gift he or she had. It is good to set aside some time to share with each other some incidents involving that friend, especially times in the group together.

Perhaps some of the most basic of all small group rituals take place in the average family. At the death of a dearly loved pet, at the leaving of one home to move to another, at any time of loss for a family to create a ritual farewell together can be a growing experience.

For years, there hung on the back of my office door in Edinburgh, a large and colourful lei made of big woolly pompoms. It had been one of the most special gifts given to me at my farewell party in Melbourne. Each of my Australian colleagues had made one of these pompoms and each was quite different from the others. They had strung them together and put them round my neck to convey the warmth of their love for me. It meant a lot more to me than their more expensive, purchased gift.

With these same colleagues, some time before this, I had attended a week-long conference. It was a week where we, and the other conference participants, had grown very close to each other. We had come from all over Australia and New Zealand and had shared a great deal of ourselves with each other. A small group was made responsible for the farewell session at the end of the conference. My vivid memory of the result of that planning, was a final session where they had designed a kind of maypole, using a person as the central pole and balls of gaily coloured wool as ribbons. Music played, as we danced in and out of our maypole circle, laughing, singing, and sometimes tossing another ball of wool across the circle while keeping hold of one end ourselves. Eventually, when the music stopped, we found we had woven an enormous multi-coloured spider's web, which in some way connected each person to every other person there—and there were dozens of us! It was a tremendously high point in our feeling of togetherness after worship. The web symbolised for us the intricacies of the friendships we had begun or had deepened throughout the week. We felt one in the Spirit.

Then, suddenly, in the midst of our elation, we became aware that the colleague who had been the central pole had produced an enormous pair of scissors. He was cutting our intricate web through the middle! It sagged, and each of us was left holding the end of one strand of coloured wool. Mine was red. It dangled pathetically, in touch with no-one but me.

That symbolic act was, literally, shocking. Words of benediction rang out over our drooping shoulders and the sorry tangled mess of woollen strands that lay at our feet. But the voice urged us to take our long strand of wool back home, remembering that of which it had once been part. We were told that, from now on, our feeling of community with each other would have no visible presence but that it must be transformed into whatever each of us would now make of it, where we normally lived and worked.

Many of us wept, for suddenly we had been made to face up to the pain of possible loneliness. We had a chance to begin to work through our grief towards a new life beyond the conference. The conference had not been an end in itself. It had been a training event to better equip us for work and service ahead. We were left facing our work, rather than looking back with nostalgia for the days we had left behind. We had experienced a goodbye.

An Exercise

For you to think through by yourself, or to share with others

1. *Have you any memories to share of rituals when pets were buried?*

2. *Spend some time with your spouse or a close friend, sharing together your wishes for your funerals/memorial services.*
   Decide together what to do with this information after you have discussed it.

3. *If you are ever in the position of supporting a relative or friend through the period before their death, consider*

Is it appropriate to ask this person to plan, with your support, the kind of funeral/memorial service he or she would like to have?

Which guidelines would you have before you as you made this decision?

4. If you know that you are soon to face some experience of loss, spend some time thinking creatively about a form of ritual which would help you let go of what you have at present, by saying a positive goodbye.

CHAPTER THIRTEEN

The regressive stage

After the stages of shock and control, the grief process moves to the regressive phase. During the time when a mourner is feeling the full force of the regressive phase, he or she may well appear to be coping with life again. The feelings of this stage can often be tightly controlled so that only those close to the mourner can guess or know what is going on inside.

At the news of any great loss, there are usually friends and relatives who will gather around to give help, comfort and support. Sooner or later, and inevitably, however, the time comes when such loving concern dwindles. Life has returned to normal for most of those involved through caring. They are back at work or back looking after the children, having done what they could in the emergency. But for those at the centre of the loss, life will never be the same again. With support gone, they are left to their own devices and there is little to cushion them then from the effects of the loss. Overwhelming, devasting feelings can begin to sweep over them. Life seems to have fallen to pieces. Some feel that the future will hold nothing but empty blackness from that point on. Some fear they will go crazy.

One Scottish factory closed down in the month of November, with the loss of 400 jobs. By April of the following year, eight of the redundant workers were dead. Some had taken their own lives in deliberate suicide; others had died as the result of excessive drinking.

With bereaved people, this 'regressive' stage in the grief

process generally happens soon after the funeral. To 'regress' is to go backwards. When this word is used in psychology, it indicates that a person seems to have gone back to a much younger stage to act at that stage again. Regression may even go as far back as childhood or infancy. Every adult human being seems to have within their personality, the child he or she once was. But it is only occasionally, in our culture, that this child is allowed to be seen in action by others and show its raw feelings, its desires and its needs clamouring for attention.

In the regressive phase of grief, this child within can be the most dominant part of the personality.

Grown-up people are used to being in charge of their feelings, and are used to having some control over what happens in their lives. If something happens that is not according to their plans or wishes, they are used to going to a doctor, a lawyer, or an insurance firm as these have the special power to make things right again. But in a situation of tragic loss, there is no human being with sufficient power to restore that which is lost. If a loved one dies, if a person's love for another dies, if a limb is cut off, if a job is lost in a time of high unemployment, the mourner is helpless.

The regressive phase of grief can be like travelling alone through a howling, evil wilderness, with no signposts to mark the way. In this wilderness, fellow travellers try to communicate but, sometimes, their language makes no sense.

The Book of Psalms describes again and again the intensity of feeling that can come over a person at this stage.

> *My God, my God, why have you abandoned me?*
> *I have cried desperately for help,*
>   *but still it does not come.*
> *During the day I call to you, my God,*
>   *but you do not answer;*
> *I call at night,*
>   *but get no rest.*

Psalm 22 : 1, 2 (GNB)

In times of trouble I pray to the Lord;
all night long I lift my hands in prayer,
but I can find no comfort.

I spend the night in deep thought;
I meditate, and this is what I ask myself:
'Will the Lord always reject us?
Will he never again be pleased with us?
Has he stopped loving us?
Does his promise no longer stand?
Has God forgotten to be merciful?
Has anger taken the place of his compassion?'
Then I said, 'What hurts me most is this—
that God is no longer powerful.'

Psalm 77 : 2, 6–10 (GNB)

Ada

Ada's experience is not uncommon. Her husband, Grant, and she had been very keen members of the local church. Together they had led a house group. Grant was killed outright in a car crash. For the first few weeks Ada was very bright. 'I feel certain that everyone is praying for me. I'm getting the strength to go on—in fact, I'm amazed by it all. I had no idea that the people in the church cared so much. Especially the house group. Every evening at least one of them phones or drops in,' she told her minister when he called to see her a fortnight after Grant's funeral.

The members of the house-group were genuinely concerned about Ada, but one by one they became convinced that she was being upheld, that she was experiencing God's presence in a special way. One by one they called less frequently, because, being busy people, they had families and others to care for too, now that Ada's crisis seemed to have passed.

It was about that time that Ada's sense of being surrounded by love and concern began to abate and the pain and loneliness of her loss hit her. If she had phoned her friends in the house-group, they would have rallied around again, but she could not bring herself to ask for help. Somehow, she felt that there must be something wrong with her faith that she no longer felt upheld and conscious of God's presence. Each time she took out her Bible to find comfort, she found herself weeping instead.

It had taken Ada about a month to reach the regressive phase in her grief. When it came, she was totally unprepared for it.

Ada had two teenage children, both still at school, and a part-time job as a sales assistant in a large chain store in the city. Very few of the customers knew her personally and so they had no idea of the experience through which she was passing. Somehow, for most of the time, at work, Ada was able to put on a bright face. She was able to respond to her customers much as she always had, except that her concentration seemed to have taken a knock. Occasionally she gave back the wrong change. Sometimes her mind went blank if she was asked if certain items were available in other sizes or colours. But she seemed to get through each day at the store. There were no reminders there of Grant.

At home, while the children were around, she was conscious of the way their grieving affected their moods, and she did her best to take care of them. The bad times for Ada were the times when her children were off to youth club, or late at night, when they had gone to bed. She had no desire to read or to sew. Television programmes held no interest for her; those she might have been interested in required too much effort or concentration. When she went to bed, sleep would not come, although she felt completely drained. When she dozed, she would often waken in the middle of a horrifying dream. She lost weight, and began to have headaches.

Recalling that time now, Ada freely admits that for two or three months her life seemed like a nightmare. Her times at work, and her knowledge that her children needed her kept her sane. She continued to attend church, but when she did, she felt as if it was not really her sitting there, but someone else acting out her role in life. There were times too when she seemed to have no feeling. There were others when the ache of her longing for Grant seemed to be a physical pain or when anger at God for allowing this to happen, almost choked her. She could not stop believing in God, but her faith was no comfort to her. Her world had gone grey. Like so many other widows, she had to struggle on as best she could.

As you read on through the other chapters about the regressive stage, remember that mourners may not be sharing any of these bad feelings and experiences with those around them. People generally feel greatly helped when they have support throughout this stage, when they have someone to whom they can turn for a listening ear—someone who cares.

CHAPTER FOURTEEN

'What is real?'

'What is "real"?' asked a toy rabbit of a toy skin horse.*

Back came the reply, 'Real isn't how you're made. It's a thing that happens to you when a child loves you for a long, long time, not just to play with, but really loves you, then you become real.'

When you lose someone who really loves you, you can feel 'unreal'. The normality of life—the reality we have taken for granted until the crisis comes—crumbles, as we try to grasp it back again. The reality we are left with is not the reality we want. Until then, we have relied on our senses of sight, hearing, smell, taste and touch, to convey to us what is 'real'.

Things commonly happen in grief that cannot be measured according to our normal standards of assessing reality.

A man whose wife had died, sensed her presence one evening. He 'knew' that she was standing behind him, just as she so often had, to read the newspaper over his shoulder. He reached up his hand to touch her. He felt nothing, yet he fancied he caught a whiff of the perfume she used to use.

Another widower looked up one evening to see his late wife, sitting across from him in the armchair by the fireplace. He was so terrified that he ran from the room and refused ever to enter it again.

A young mother of two children under the age of two had lost her mother, with whom she had been very close. One

*The Velveteen Rabbit, by Margery Williams (Heinemann)

afternoon she felt exhausted. Both babies were crying, and whatever she did, nothing seemed to comfort them. At last she had had enough. She carried both children through to their bedroom, laid them, still protesting vehemently, in their cots, and closed the door firmly behind her. She made herself a cup of tea and sat down on an easy chair to try to relax.

Then she thought she heard the bedroom door open. 'It felt as if my mother was going into the room to look after my babies for me,' she said afterwards. 'I felt so relieved. They stopped crying, and I felt she had picked them up and was carrying them around the room. I relaxed and knew everything would be alright.'

It is comparatively common for those who have lost a spouse to waken in the night and feel their late partner in bed with them or standing by the bed, smiling, or saying something to them. Sometimes widows and widowers report having long conversations at such times. One friend told me that he had had such an experience on several occasions, the most recent being a time when his late wife had discussed with him his forthcoming re-marriage.

Loving Touch

During the Second World War a young nurse became engaged to a young man in the R A F she described him to me as 'not handsome, but with lovely twinkling eyes. He was great fun.'

She was nursing in Glasgow, coping with the awful aftermath of the Clydebank blitz, when she got the news that his plane had come down, and he, though still alive, had been 'a living torch' in the wreckage. She was allowed to visit him in hospital in England. He was swathed in bandages—in her words, 'There was not a place where I could kiss him. Only his eyes were visible.' He died a week later.

Nine months later she had been working overtime on ship-loads of prisoners home from prisoner-of-war camps in the

Far East when she felt a physical pain grow inside her in reaction to the suffering to which she was exposed. One day when she was off-duty she knelt down in her room and cried out, 'Why, God? Why all this terrible suffering?' The physical pain left her, and in its place, came a sense of peace.

Three years after her fiancé's death she formed a close relationship with another man but all the time she was with him she felt that somehow she was betraying the first man by growing to love the new one.

One evening her new boyfriend asked her to marry him. She was facing him and his arms were clasped round her back. Just then, over his shoulder, she saw her first fiancé, healed and smiling, close enough for her to touch had she reached out to him. He was saying (without words) that it was all right to accept—that there was no betrayal. She did say 'yes'!

Spina Bifida

A woman in her forties whose family was almost ready to leave the nest, discovered she was pregnant. Her baby was born with *spina bifida* and lived only a day or two in intensive care. A few days later the mother had an experience in which the baby came to her and said, 'Mummy, I'll never leave you. I'll look after you now. All the others will grow up and leave you but I will always be with you.'

Such strange experiences do not only come to those who are overwrought at the time or who have vivid imaginations, or those who are highly susceptible to suggestion. They come to people who are grieving, to help them work through their grief. Occasionally they will come through other people.

One night a minister was called to a home where the news had come through that both parents had been killed outright in a car crash. He waited with one teenage son till he heard the other return home. He went towards the lad to tell him the news, only to hear him say, 'I know. They're dead, aren't they.

What happened?' He went on to explain to his minister that he had been at a party when, out of the blue, he had had the conviction that both his parents were dead. At once he left, and came home. The 'conviction' about his parents had come to him, not at the time of the crash, but a few hours later.

During the years that followed, the minister grew close to both the bereaved brothers as he gave them what support he could. Then the time came when his own mother was seriously ill. Before she died, she lay in a coma for a week. During that time, she responded only to touch—groaning as they turned her on her bed, lying peacefully when someone held her hand. She died, having been unable to say goodbye to her family.

Three minutes after she died, the manse telephone rang. It was the lad who had 'known' that his own parents had died. 'How's your mother?' he asked the minister. 'She died a few minutes ago,' he told him. 'I thought so,' the young man replied. 'She appeared right beside me and gave me a message, which I'm certain she meant me to give to you.' 'When was that?' enquired the minister. 'Just a few minutes ago,' came the answer. 'Can I read it to you?'

He read:

> *My day is setting, and as the twilight grows,*
> *I must go gently on.*
> *I am at one.*

The minister (who happened to be a graduate both in science and in theology) felt greatly comforted. Through those few lines, his mother, who loved to read poetry, had said goodbye to him.

Many people have experiences similar to these—happenings they cannot explain. Most seem to find these reassuring. Some are extremely disturbed by them. More common, and very understandable, is that which is experienced by most people when a friend or relative dies. They think they see him or her on a passing bus or in a crowd in a street, only to have the pang of realising that they must be mistaken. I know one girl who ran after a man she took to be her father and grabbed him by the arm. When he turned round, she was confronted by a total stranger.

Sharing and Responding

People are often very hesitant to share these experiences because they do not accord with our normal way of assessing reality. They say, 'I suppose I must have been imagining it!' or 'I'd like to tell you something, but I don't know what to make of it . . .' Sometimes they will end with, 'Do you think I was dreaming?' or even, 'Am I going a bit crazy?' If those with whom they attempt to share have had no such experience for themselves, the listeners can become extremely alarmed. If they do not know that such experiences are relatively common, they *can* imagine that the one who is recounting them has temporarily 'lost the place, or is claiming to believe in ghosts or is dabbling in spiritualism. Their fear can make them very rejecting and scornful of those who have shared something intimate with them.

If you are privileged to listen to someone who chooses to share such an experience with you, listen to it with great respect. It is something which cannot be explained satisfactorily as yet because of our limited knowledge. It is not helpful in such a situation to respond, 'You must have felt reassured/ comforted/scared/bewildered (or whatever) when that happened.' People react in so many possible ways, that your selection of one that they *must* have felt might be quite inappropriate. It is usually much more helpful to respond, 'How did you feel after that experience?' and to accept whatever the person says as how it was for him or her.

It is good to be able to give reassurance that such experiences are said to occur to about half of all people who are suffering from a close bereavement.

'That hesitant Conversation'

We are so used to communicating with those who are meaningful to us while they are alive, that it would be odd if all trace of this were to vanish immediately on their death. Earlier, I mentioned that my mother had died while I was working in Australia. I flew home for her funeral, then came home again to work in Scotland a few months later. I greatly missed the chats we had always had. Every Sunday while I was away, I had written a long letter home telling my parents what I had been doing. I could not get used to not being able to communicate with her.

One day in late summer, I went off alone to her grave. It was a warm, peaceful afternoon. The graveyard is on a grassy hillside with a beautiful view over an island bay and there was nobody else in sight. I sat down on the grass that covered her grave, as I had sat so often years before, on her knee, and I talked to her. She was always a superb listener. I told her what had been happening to me over the months since her death. I told her how I was feeling. I cried quietly as I talked and I felt she was understanding me, as she always had. I was not attempting to get any 'message from the other side'. I was allowing myself to re-experience the loving understanding stored in my memory of her. On that occasion I sorely needed the experience of feeling physically close to her again and I got it. Always, when I had come home, she had been there for me. I needed to readjust before I could cope with her absence.

Alastair Reid wrote a poem entitled, 'My Father, Dying.' Near its end he writes:

> *I am not ready*
> *to be without your frail and wasted body,*
> *your miscellaneous mind-way . . .*

and then goes on to say

> *But on any one*
> *of these nights soon,*
> *for you, the dark will not crack with dawn,*
>
> *and then I will begin*
> *with you that hesitant conversation*
> *going on and on and on.*

From very early years we are able to have conversations inside our head with people we know well. We know what they might say to us, in any given situation, and we carry this knowledge around with us. We are able to do this while our friends and relatives are still alive, and we do not lose the ability if they die, or if we travel to the other end of the world without them. If it is appropriate, I will often ask a grieving person, 'Do you ever talk to him/her?' Often the response is a shy smile, and a 'Well, yes. I do.' If, instead, it is a look of alarm or of blank amazement, I will share my own experience, and the comfort I found through it. Very often I will also explain my belief that it is part of a loving God's provision for our needs, and that it is a little bit of what we mean by 'the communion of saints' although it can be understood in terms of human memory.

Since that time when I sat on my mother's grave, and felt I was talking to her, I have occasionally revisited the spot. But I no longer need to feel her presence there. I do still, in my imagination, chat a little to her now and then. I have no trouble imagining what she might reply! Nowadays, its fun. I laugh at myself when I do it.

And so, what do *you* think? What is 'real'?

An Exercise

For you to share with others in a group.

Have you had any experience similar to those mentioned in this chapter? Have you come across any experienced by others?

If you feel like sharing any such experience, do so. As you do, let the others in your small group respond to what you share, helping you to talk and to explore what it means to you.

CHAPTER FIFTEEN

Moving through dreams

Julie was twelve when she came to live with my husband and me from the children's home where she had lived happily for more than five years. During the months when adjusting to her new surroundings was difficult, she had several dreams which were a sheer delight to her. In each of them, Puff, the Magic Dragon would come to her new bedroom. With her younger brother, she would hop on to his back and they would fly north across the broad river estuary, right into the bedroom she used to share with her older sister in the children's home. No adult in either home would be aware of the wonderful escapades in which the reunited children were involved, though there was at least one occasion in the dream when the staff of the home was wakened by the noise of the frolics, and Julie and her brother had to hide while they came to investigate!

Now, more than a year later, that series of dreams remains as a happy memory.

Reassurance

Lindsay's mother died of cancer, supported and surrounded by her loving husband, married children and their families. I asked Lindsay to record her experience of a dream after her mother's death, and she wrote, 'My last actual visual memory of her after she died isn't a good one: the nurses moved in to do the needful as we were leaving and the door to her single room was not closed as I looked back and saw that they'd already taken off her wig . . .'

'The dream I had about Mummy after she died must have

lasted only seconds but the feeling of reality behind it was *so* powerful. The family were all staying at my parents' home. We had all been out for a walk, which included going to the swing park for the kids. On coming back in, my sister and I went into the living room. There was Mummy, sitting in her usual chair, knitting. She looked up as we came in, and I could see that she was *well*—looking years younger—and she had her own hair! I said something like, 'You look marvellous!' and she said: 'I am. I'm completely better. Isn't it great?' Then we hugged each other—and the dream ended with the rest of the family coming in and joining in the hugging! I was left feeling very happy.'

'In the dream, Mummy was doing something she often used to, in life, on a wintry day—she preferred to stay in and knit if it was cold, even when she was well. The cancer was definitely acknowledged in the dream and she had completely overcome it—even to the extent of growing back the lovely brown hair she had before she was ill, and which she lost through chemotherapy.'

Lindsay felt tremendously reassured and comforted after that dream.

Keeping in touch with how the Loss feels

Jean had been aware of the reported dangers of cigarette smoking for some time, but it was not until she had an early morning visit to the dentist in which he bluntly said 'You stink of cigarette smoke!' that she made the decision to break the habit. She had been smoking from about twelve to twenty cigarettes a day at that point. She cut down her consumption and on St Valentine's Day, 1980, threw her last cigarette end on the fire. But as she stopped, a series of dreams began.

In the first few dreams, Jean was conscious that there were cigarettes around. She would be offered one, but would refuse, saying, 'I've stopped smoking.' From there, she went to dreams in which she would have a cigarette in her hand. Her husband would say, 'Don't smoke!' to which she would reply, 'I'm not going to. I'm just pretending.' After that, dreams would come in which she not only held the cigarette in her hand, but she would light it and take a puff. For a second she would feel euphoric, but her bliss was short-lived. Guilt would sweep through her, and she would throw the newly-lit cigarette down and grind it into the earth. She would become aware that her hair stank of smoke and she would attempt to get rid of the smell so that no-one would know.

These dreams continued for around four years after she had stopped smoking. She has not had such a dream for over a year now, although she confesses that she still feels that she wants a smoke each time she sees someone else have their first puff on a fresh cigarette!

Letting Pain surface

After I had the experience of giving two dearly loved little foster sons to prospective adoptive parents, it was some time before I allowed myself to grieve. Eventually, although I could control myself by not thinking about them during the day, my unconscious began to make me pay attention to the loss through a series of nightmares. All I could remember when I awoke was that I had had yet another horrific dream in which the younger of the two boys had had something fearful happen to him—he had died or was dreadfully hurt and suffering.

In my waking hours I began to grieve more openly and consciously, realising my need for this. At long last I had a dream which is still vivid in my memory. In it, I was standing beside a deep river, watching the grey water flow powerfully by. Then I saw the little boy's body, face downwards, floating downstream in the current. I knew he was dead but I had to get to him. I waded out, waist-deep into the river, and caught up his body as it floated past me. Instantly he came alive in my arms, chuckling up into my face and throwing his arms around me, just as he had done so often in reality when we played together.

That dream marked for me, the turning point in my grief for him. Years later I still now and then dream of him and of his elder brother, but since that point the dreams have been happy ones. It no longer hurts to remember them.

Struggling against Denial

Victoria was in her fifties when her husband died of a sudden heart-attack. At the beginning, her struggle to adjust to the reality of her loss was reflected in her dreams. In those dreams his physical presence was so real that she could reach out and hold on to his shoulders and grip his hands. It was not dream-like for Victoria—he was *there*—just as surely as ever he had been before his death. Waking to face the shocking reality of her loss once more, seemed to be repeating, over and over, her initial shock and horror at the news of his death. As time went by, the dreams focused more on his general presence in and around their house. She would dream that she came home to see his keys in the door, and think, 'He's *home*! What a nightmare it has all been! How wonderful to be able to tell everyone it isn't true after all!' But the overwhelming feeling of relief was shattered when she woke to be confronted with reality again. Each time she experienced such a dream she would feel distressed and weepy for the rest of the day. Now, four years later, in her dreams, she will see him working in the garage, or doing something around the house, and she can say to herself. 'This is nice, but I'm dreaming it.'

Neither asleep nor awake does she now deny that he is no longer with her. She does not now experience the intense, overwhelming joy in her dreams of believing he is alive again, but neither does she sink to the same distressing depths of pain on waking up to face life as it is.

Listening to Dreams

If you come across people in the regressive phase of grief who are having recurrent disturbing dreams, encourage them to talk with you about their dreams. Remember that the dreams are *their* dreams: they are not *your* dreams! At best, (unless you are a trained dream analyst) if you attempt to interpret their dreams, all you can do is to guess what *your* unconscious might have been saying to *you* if *you* had had that dream.

Dreams usually present the dreamer with pictures he or she needs to see. As the dreamer begins to pay attention to the message of the dream, the need for the dream may lessen or disappear. The skills the supporting friend requires, are generally not those of interpretation, but of caring listening, and the ability to ask helpful questions. Helpful questions are those which invite the dreamer to look at what he or she has been avoiding in conscious thought, so that the unconscious had to present it in the form of a dream. So, if you are with a person who has had an upsetting dream, first invite him or her to tell you about the dream. When you know the story, you might ask a question like: 'What do you suspect that dream was about?' or 'What was that dream telling you, that you need to know?'

The details the dreamer remembers will probably have significance for him, although he may not be able to identify it right away. Having listened carefully to the details as they are told to you, ask about the meaning of each. Here are some examples:

'You say you found yourself standing in an empty house. How did that feel to you at the time?'

'You mentioned that the windows were wide open. Why were they wide open in your dream?'

'I noticed that in the dream you felt that the baby fell because you weren't holding it properly. You felt that it was your fault. Why did you need to feel guilty in your dream?'

'You said that at one point you knew your mother was there, although you couldn't see her. Why was she there just then?'

If the dreamer cannot answer your question, it may be that what you have asked is irrelevant. It could also be that you have put your finger on something that the person's conscious mind does not yet want to look at. Either way, it is best not to press a question which appears to be leading nowhere. Some of the questions you will ask will probably receive a direct answer, like 'The windows were open because he was free to go.' You can follow that up with, 'Does that make sense to you?' Normally, if a person has given even a tentative interpretation, it will make sense to him or her. It does not need to make sense to the listener as long as it makes sense to the dreamer.

If you feel that the dreamer is getting nowhere with attempts to interpret a dream, stop asking questions. It may be that he will have another, similar dream, before he is willing to look at what he needs to. It could equally well be that he or she has realised the significance of the dream, but for some reason is unwilling to share more with you.

I have found that when people have been helped to explore a bad dream which has to do with loss, one of two things is likely to follow. Either they do not have another similar disturbing dream, because the issue it raised has been faced or else the talking is followed by another dream in which the nightmare situation resolves itself.

Saying Goodbye in Dreams

Win was a doctor with a young family of her own when her father died. Although she had been with him regularly during his final illness, she did not see him after his death. She made the arrangements, as he had wished, for his body to be taken to the Anatomy Department at a local teaching hospital. Since there was no body to necessitate a funeral, a memorial service was held for him.

Some time after this—in fact, around the second anniversary of his death—Win began to have a series of nightmares. The common theme of these was of her search for his body. In one particularly vivid one, Win was in a park full of faceless people who were sitting on benches or walking around. In the dream, Win rushed round the park, certain that her father was there. He was somewhere, but she was quite unable to find him. Sometimes she thought she saw him, but when she turned the persons around, they were strangers. Her panic at not being able to find him was very real to her, even after she had wakened.

In another dream, everything had been dark and enclosed. It felt to her as if nothing could escape from where she was.

In part of a conversation I had with Win about other matters, she told me about those dreams. She felt they were coming because she had not been able to say goodbye to her father and so was clinging to her grief, instead of letting him go. It was a very sad part of our conversation, but it was not a counselling situation, so I did not invite Win to say goodbye to her father there and then.

A week later we had to meet again on other business. 'You'll never guess what happened!' she exclaimed, smiling very happily. 'I had another dream about my Dad. He was there!' she said. 'His body was lying on *my* bed, in *my* home. All the windows were wide open—even the skylight on the roof. The sun was shining—streaming in through all the windows, filling the room with light and air, and the birds were singing. There was only one thing wrong—and that was that I knew I mustn't go and tell my mother about it—and she was downstairs at the time. And then everything became just perfect, because I knew that she knew too.'

So Win had found what she had been searching for. More than a year has passed since then, and she has not dreamed of

him since. With that dream, she found him, said goodbye and
let him go.

An Exercise

For you to think through by yourself, or discuss with others
1. *Have you ever had a dream (or a series of dreams) when you
   were suffering from loss? If so, what did that dream mean
   for you?*
2. *If anyone in your group would like to share the story of a
   dream he or she had after a loss, help that person to think
   through the dream, following the pattern suggested in this
   chapter.*

CHAPTER SIXTEEN

It's difficult to think straight

'I don't know what's the matter with me!' 'I didn't think.' 'I don't seem to be able to help myself.' Phrases like that often come from the lips of people in the regressive stage of grief. Problems they would normally handle easily can seem too much trouble to think through. Friends supporting them will sometimes be completely taken aback because they see them acting out of character. They will want to say, 'But why on earth did you do that?' or 'But surely that's not reasonable. Why are you blaming yourself?' They feel as if the mourners are deliberately turning their backs on the resources of logical common sense they normally use. Grieving people can feel as if they can't get through to these sources of energy and wisdom.

Complete Regression

Occasionally the regressive stage of grief is so severe that complete institutional care has to be given to him or her. This is necessary because the person has ceased to look after him or herself in a responsible manner. A person in this condition may for instance, turn her face to the wall, quite literally, and refuse to eat or rise from her bed. Another may be drunk for days on end.

A complete regression of this kind is usually temporary, and the person concerned can be given professional help and will pull through it.

Decision-making at the Regressive Stage

Healthy decision-making involves the ability to think through the consequences of the decision in a logical and reasonable manner. This logical process neither overlooks needs and feelings nor responsibilities and ethical standards. It takes all these into account. Thus the decision is made in the setting of long-term needs and objectives and within the context of the other people who have to be considered. But the pain and upset of the regressive stage can be so severe that all the sufferer can think to do, is to make it stop. Decisions—even ones that involve long-term relationships or major expense—can be made with feelings or needs in control. 'I will have this, because I want it or need it now! If I have it, the pain will go away.' (The 'it' may be a new home or a new spouse or a new job, etc.)

Alex and Ann

Alex had been very dependent on Katie, his capable and motherly young wife. If it had not been for his wife's friend, Ann, he could never have kept his young family together through the final awful months of Katie dying of cancer. When Katie did die, Ann moved back to her own flat. She took the children when Alex needed this, but she was not always there for him to turn to, and he found it increasingly difficult to cope with all the needs of the children and the housework, along with his own needs.

After Katie's death, Ann, too found it difficult to pick up her life where she had left it, before she had moved in to help. She missed the children especially, and she desperately missed being needed by Alex and Katie. Her life suddenly felt empty and pointless.

Three months after their bereavement, Alex and Ann decided to get married. It looked like a decision that would solve the problems for everyone and take away the pain. It solved a few problems right away, but it brought a great many more as the months went by and the regressive phase of their grief for Katie receded. If they had managed to live through the pain without marrying each other, eventually they would both have chosen different partners, much more suited to their long-term needs.

Graeme and Hamish

Graeme was the treasurer at his parish church. His wife, Sheila, had a very severe stroke. During her illness, he gave up all other outside interests apart from his church duty. He did not want to keep that on and did not particularly enjoy the work, but when he had tried to give it up, nobody else volunteered to take it over because of the responsibility involved.

Over the months, Hamish, one of his fellow elders, was watching him, full of pity and concern, but not knowing what he could do to help. One Sunday, Hamish was on duty, counting the offering with Graeme. As they finished off, Hamish heard Graeme give a deep sigh. He looked up and caught an exhausted, strained look on his friend's face.

Hamish: Things are really hard for you these days, aren't they, Graeme?

Graeme: I don't like to admit it I suppose, but yes, they are. I haven't the energy I used to have.

Hamish: Do you have a break from it all, apart from when you are at work?

Graeme: Well, this is my break. I still get to church each week. Sheila can't come to the service, so she's at home by herself while I'm here. We don't get help at the weekends.

Hamish: Is that the only time you have?

Graeme: Look, I think I know what you're getting at, but I can't be selfish. She can't enjoy herself, so why should I?

Hamish: Graeme, you always say that you're a man who calls a spade a spade. I'd like to be frank with you.

Graeme: What do you mean? Oh well, go on then.

Hamish: It seems to me that you're probably not very good company for Sheila if you're as strained and tired as you sound and look. (At this point, Hamish put his hand on Graeme's shoulder.)

There was silence. Graeme seemed near to tears.

Graeme: You're right. I'm not.

Hamish: What would you really love to do for a few hours, Graeme, if you didn't have Sheila to look after?

Graeme: Hmm . . . a pipe dream . . . You know, I suppose I'd just love to take a walk in the hills, and let the wind blow on my face again, but . . .

Hamish: But nothing! I've an idea that it would do Sheila the world of good to feel she wasn't trapping you at home, and to have a husband that was feeling more like his old self again. Look, Barbara and I are free next Saturday. We could take Sheila out somewhere in her wheelchair . . .

Graeme was in the regressive phase of his grief at Sheila's sudden paralysis. He was doing his very best to look after Sheila at the cost of looking after himself. Since enjoyment had gone from her life, he felt guilty if he enjoyed his. Sometimes, although he could not have shared this with anyone, he even wished that Sheila had died instead of being left paralysed. But he could not fail in his duty towards her.

He had not been able to look at what this was doing to his own personality and at how that would inevitably affect Sheila. It had not even dawned on him that she might like to have the company of others apart from himself, the home help and the nurse, on some occasions. Graeme was punishing himself— and her—instead of talking things over with someone who could be more objective in the situation. He needed Hamish to come alongside him. Hamish's caring allowed Graeme to free himself from an over-severe sense of duty. And in the end, Sheila benefited too.

Decision-making in the regressive phase of the grief process is therefore likely not to be functioning well.

If you have reason to believe that a person you care for is under some stress in a loss situation—especially during the few months immediately after their loss has occurred, get alongside that person, as Hamish did. Help that person to talk through what is happening in his or her life and any plans that are under consideration. If you think that what is being said is not going to be a balanced, long-term solution to the present pain, then do not hesitate to ask questions like: 'So you're going to put your house on the market, and go to live with your son and his wife in Wales. Have you many close friends who live near them? What arrangements are you making for when you want some privacy? etc.'

If you feel you are being given glib answers which indicate to you that the person has not considered all the factors which would have to be taken into account, then do not be afraid to say so. You can risk offending that person for a few minutes, or even hours or a couple of days, but that is infinitely better than allowing your friend to go ahead with a decsion that might make the rest of her life a misery. It is possible to say, 'I want to say something to you that you might find unacceptable . . . I know that while you stay in this house you are constantly surrounded with painful memories of your husband, and that must be very sore for you. But I feel that if you sell this house and move away now, you are running away from it all, rather than facing up to your grief. How about waiting for a few months before you make the decision about selling this house? I think you may feel quite differently about it after a while.'

Often we Christians do not love our neighbours as we love ourselves and so we do not risk confronting them. Confrontation might be slightly easier for you if you realise that at the regressive phase in grief, pain can blind your neighbour to what seems only too obvious to you. You would not allow a blind person to fall over an obstacle which you could see, because you did not like to interfere!

Trying to stop people like Alex and Ann from marrying can be a very tricky thing indeed! People often have very successful marriages with partners their friends would think highly unsuitable for them! Again, do what you can to help them see the wisdom of waiting till the worst pain of grieving is lived through before they make a legal commitment to each other. If their need for each other stems from their grief, it will lessen, naturally and gradually, once the regressive phase of grief passes.

A Warning to those who give Advice

If you arrive in a situation where your friends decide against selling a house, or changing a job, or delaying a marriage just because you have told them to do this, watch out! The most likely thing to happen will be that, if something goes wrong, the blame will be laid squarely at your door. 'But you made me do that!' 'It's all your fault!' 'If it hadn't been for you, I would now be . . .' And your friends will have every justification for doing that to you! Your support ought to help them think through the consequences for themselves rather than telling them what you think the consequences might be.

Do be as certain as you can that you are able to be objective in your help. If you have a vested interest in what they decide, you, also, might be operating out of your needs and fears.

An Exercise

For you to think through by yourself, or with others

1. *Have you ever had an experience when you were so overcome with emotion that you were not thinking straight? (The emotion may have been a happy one like falling in love. It could equally well be one like having a fit of temper, or feeling extreme jealousy or any other strong feeling.) If you have, what was the feeling? What did you do or think, that you now believe was an odd way to behave?*

2. *If you were listening to someone who had been through a severe loss, and that person told you of a plan that you thought was unwise, what could you do about it? If you can think of an actual situation, consider what could be an appropriate action for you to take.*

CHAPTER SEVENTEEN

Don't be scared of anger!

Somewhere during my childhood I picked up the notion that Job's greatness lay in the fact that, although he was sorely tried, he was never angry. Reading the Book of Job as an adult, I discovered that this was far from the truth. Job soundly cursed the day of his birth and he was rightly furious at the kind of comfort his friends offered him. He did not express his anger directly at God, although he seems to come pretty close to that now and then.

Were you brought up, as I was, to believe that Christians must never, never be angry unless what they felt was 'righteous indignation'? If you were, you might be afraid of anger too: afraid enough to demand that modern believers around you do not show it.

Have a look for a moment at a different believer—one of the Psalmists whose words are not too often read out in comforting services, at least not with the force of hurt anger in which they must have been written.

An Exercise

> *Turn to Psalm 44 in a modern version.*
>> *Verses 1–8 make comfortable reading . . .*
>>> *but have a look at verses 9 to 25!!!*
>> *How would you feel if you had to read these out at a church service?*
>> *Imagine the effect this would have on an average congregation if it was delivered by a powerful actor who was allowed full*

*dramatic license! Can you hear him scream into the echoing
silence 'Wake up, Lord! Why are you asleep? Rouse yourself!
Don't reject us for ever!'*

I think I would feel embarrassed if that happened! I would
probably want to cover it up a bit by saying; 'Of course, the
Psalmist had a limited picture of God, you know . . . a pre-
Christian concept . . .' But if I had stood at the foot of the
cross on that Friday, and heard the cry, 'My God, my God,
why did you abandon me?' . . . would I have had words to
rationalise that? God does not demand that his children bow
their heads and suffer in silence! What he may ask, is silence
from those who listen to the screams of anger and hurt and
despair.

Anger is *not* forbidden in scripture. Here is what it says in
Ephesians 4:26: 'If you become angry, do not let your anger
lead you into sin, and do not stay angry all day.' (GNB)

Anger is a healthy reaction to loss

'Why did God take my baby?' 'What have I done to deserve
this?' 'How can a loving God allow the father of five little
children to be killed in Ulster?' 'I'm going to sue that doctor!'
'How can you stand there, claiming to believe in God, when
my wife was burned to death trying to save a drunken lout?'
'Why did you leave me? I can't live without you!' 'Him? He
died to spite me!' 'I've no use for God now. I prayed . . . I
wasted my breath!'

Anger is not meant to be bottled up

Anger, in mourning, is a big cover-up for helplessness. If
the anger is not allowed to come out, it can be bottled up, and
gradually turn into sour bitterness which can warp a personality
and damage relationships with God, as well as with other

human beings. Mourners who cannot express anger sometimes grow depressed and withdraw from the relationships they could have with those alive and round about them. They use the anger to punish themselves instead of using it to come to terms with their loss.

Unexpressed anger can be stored up in the body and lead to physical illness.

Dr Elisabeth Kübler-Ross, is one of the world's greatest teachers in the field of death and dying. For many years now she has helped countless terminally ill people face up to their death in a very positive and healthy way. As her clients tackle the task of acknowledging the loss of their own lives, most go through a time of experiencing anger. 'Why me? There's still so much I want to do with my life! I'm too young to die!' Rather than bottle up these feelings or have them come out against those caring for them, Kübler-Ross recommends that the angry feelings should be expressed. She gives her clients a length of rubber hose pipe, and encourages them to use it to discharge their anger on, for instance, a cushion, and to yell and scream their anger out as they do this.

When anger is allowed to be verbally expressed in mourning, it often dissolves in tears. The tears express the helplessness hidden below the anger. With a caring friend it can be safe enough to feel the helplessness.

Anger can be frightening

The trouble with the angry phase of grief is that it generally frightens those who come around to give support and comfort!

An Exercise

Think yourself into this situation

Imagine that you are visiting a friend two weeks after her baby has died. Without warning she blurts out; 'Oh why did God do it? If He's supposed to be a Father, then He must have known how I would feel! Then He's cruel! He's not loving!'

1. How would you feel at that moment?
2. What would you be likely to say or do in that situation?

You might feel scared, confused—as if you and God were under attack. Your spontaneous reaction might be to say something to defend either God, or yourself, or both! Your friend might then feel as if you had tried to put her in her place and that you had misunderstood her.

Here are a few things some people might say in that situation.

1. Oh, you mustn't feel like that!
2. But ... but He is loving! You just can't feel it right now.
3. Hush ... don't upset yourself like that!
4. But God didn't do it! There must have been some human error.
5. But God never lets us shed a needless tear, so there must be a reason somewhere. It's just that we can't see it yet. One day we will understand.

None of these replies will help an angry mourner feel safe enough to go on expressing her anger until she can let the helplessness come through. Somehow there has to be permission to express anger. That will come if she feels understood, that she is allowed to express what she is actually feeling.

So what can you do?

When you see a grieving person feeling angry, say to yourself 'This person is probably feeling lost and helpless. There's nothing she (or he) can do to change what has happened. She is scared of being in a world where such bad things can happen.

Instead of being scared too, I'm going to care for the frightened child hiding inside the anger.'

Shift your concern away from yourself so that it is free to reach out to the angry person.

It does not make a lot of sense to try to defend God at any time, because he is quite big enough to defend himself! But to try to defend God against a frightened, insecure child is the last thing the child needs! The child needs to feel God being there, understanding. If you can be there, understanding, then Christ is in you.

But while all that is going on in your mind, there, in front of you, is a very angry person. And the anger, in spite of what it is covering up, is real anger. Somehow, you have to come alongside the angry person, allowing her to be angry.

An Exercise

Look back again at the situation mentioned above, where the young mother said, 'Oh WHY did God do it? If He's supposed to be a Father, then He must have known how I would feel! Then He's cruel! He's NOT loving!'

This time, instead of thinking how YOU would feel sitting listening to her, think

1. *How is SHE feeling right now? What is SHE thinking? and then think*

2. *How can I put that in my own words, so that she will feel that I understand her at this moment and accept her need to express her thoughts and feelings?*

Each person will have his or her own words to reflect back thoughts and feelings to that young mother. Let me tell you those I might choose in that situation. I would probably say, very gently, 'You feel that God has let you down.' My sentence would be a quiet statement. It would not be a challenge to fight about whether or not God does let people down.

If I have misinterpreted what she has said, then she can

respond, 'No, you've got it wrong. What I feel is . . .' If I have picked up her thoughts and feelings correctly, then my words and attitude give her permission to go on expressing her anger in any way she chooses.

I know that some people find this kind of approach to others very difficult. Some might find it so impossible to believe that God could let someone down, that they would think they were betraying him by using the words I have suggested above. In their minds, it is wrong to reflect back such thoughts in case the other person believes that you are agreeing with what she has said. When I use this way of listening, I do not see myself as agreeing with what people are telling me, but as saying to them: 'I want to understand what you are saying. This is what I am hearing from you.'

This way of listening to other people is often called 're-flective listening'. If you use it, you are acting like a mirror for the person who is sharing thoughts and feelings, reflecting back what you see going on inside him or her. It is a supportive and uncritical way of being with people, and is particularly helpful in enabling grieving people to talk about the overwhelming and often confusing thoughts and emotions warring inside them.

The next chapter will give further help in using this technique.

A Word of Warning

There are occasions when reflective listening is not appropriate. One of these is when you see or sense that grieving persons are so overwhelmed with anger or guilt that they are likely to do damage to themselves or others. For instance, a man might attempt to drive, and do so recklessly: a mother might physically damage a child in her rage. In that kind of situation, do not encourage the expression of feelings! Do what you can to take control of the situation. Do not allow them to do things they will later regret. Get help as soon as possible and make sure you do not leave them on their own.

CHAPTER EIGHTEEN

Listening reflectively

At 86, Doris's mother was bedridden. Twice a week the district nurse called on the old lady. One day when Doris opened the door to her, it seemed to the nurse that Doris might have been crying, but she was not certain. While she attended to her patient, she was thinking with some concern, about how Doris might be feeling. On her way out, she went to speak to her.

Nurse: Well, that's that for another day, Doris. Your mother really is a grand old lady! And it means such a lot to her to be able to be looked after at home after that long spell in hospital.

Doris: Thanks, nurse. Yes, I know. She often thanks me, and ... well, it's good that I was able to retire when she needed me. If this had happened a few years ago, my pension would have suffered. It would have been so much more difficult to leave my job.

Nurse: It wasn't easy to leave your job? (RL)

Doris: No ... it's been difficult ... sometimes I miss it very much.

Nurse: What do you miss most of all, Doris?

Doris: I was always on the move, you know ... I was meeting so many people day by day ... but now ... (she shrugged her shoulders)

Nurse: Now you're stuck in the house, with only your mother for company. (RL)

Doris: That's it. It's not that I can't walk through the door and leave her for a short while ... and occasionally

my sister-in-law will come and sit with mother of an
evening and let me get out socially . . . Oh, I've really
nothing to grumble about! Just listen to me . . . full
of self-pity! Mother is so patient, and she asks so
little for herself. I'm getting so selfish! This
morning, before you came, I was giving myself a
good talking to! I realised I was thinking like a spoilt
child . . . and here I go again! (Her voice grew
sharper and she avoided the nurse's eyes.)

(The nurse clearly heard the anger in Doris's voice in this
statement. She realised that Doris felt that it was all right to
be angry with herself for being selfish, but that she probably
felt that she couldn't be angry with her mother, or at her
mother's illness for robbing her of the life she had before. The
nurse knew it was important for Doris to feel free to be angry
without having to punish herself and so make it even more
difficult for her to cope with the situation she couldn't
change.)

Nurse: You know, Doris, if I were in your shoes, I might
    (*) feel quite resentful at having to give up my job
    before I had planned to, no matter how much I loved
    my mother or felt that it was the right thing to do.

(Doris looked at the nurse for a moment, then her lip
trembled slightly. She nodded, and tried to speak, but couldn't.
She was twisting a duster round and round as she held it in
her hands. Feeling sure she was on the right wavelength, the
nurse continued . . .)

Nurse: You're *not* a spoilt child! In fact you're more like a
    good child who has suddenly been locked up in her
    (*) room with no explanation given! If that
    happened to me, I'd be angry! (And she banged her
    fist on the back of a well-padded arm-chair.)

(In response to the scene of the nurse getting so worked up

on her behalf, Doris's tension began to go, and she gave a wry smile.)

Doris: That poor old armchair! Do you know, this morning, when I was dusting, I did just what you've done. You're right. I felt so frustrated that it seemed the only thing I could vent my feelings on! (And she emphasised the words with some vehemence as she spoke—the self-pitying tone gone completely.)

Nurse: Good for you! And it looks as if it can take plenty more. The next time, when you've finished thumping the armchair, there's something else you ought to do.

Doris: What would that be?

Nurse: Make yourself a cup of tea. Sit down. Put your feet up, listen to a good record. Doctor's orders!

Doris: (laughing) You're good for me, nurse. I feel so much better for having this chat with you. I don't think I'll need to use the old armchair again for a while ... I suppose it'll take time for me to get adjusted to being at home ... thanks anyway, for understanding.

In that conversation, the nurse was listening very skilfully to Doris—not only to what she was actually saying, but to the feelings that lay below the words. If you look back at the conversation, you will see the initials 'RL' twice. These are in the places where the nurse used the technique of reflective listening. In those places, she put into her own words what Doris had indicated in what she said. This let Doris feel understood and supported.

In two other places, there is a symbol like this (*). In these places, the nurse was doing something slightly different. In our culture, many people think less of themselves if they show anger to others. The nurse could sense the anger that was being bottled up inside Doris, but if she had told her this, Doris might have felt she was being accused of having feelings she ought not to have had. By telling Doris that in her place, she would have felt resentful and angry, the nurse gave Doris permission to admit to having those feelings.

Both by using reflective listening and by offering her what she might feel in that situation, the nurse was giving Doris the opportunity to say, 'No. You've got it wrong. That's not how I feel!' if, in fact, she had been misunderstood. By the time the nurse had left therefore, Doris knew that it was natural for her to have angry feelings about being trapped by her mother's illness. The nurse had helped her to look after herself in a healthy way with the burden she had to carry. Without the nurse's good listening, Doris might have built up resentment against her mother, continued to feel guilty and punished herself for doing this. The nurse had helped Doris love both her mother and herself.

Reflective listening is a particularly useful tool to use in a situation where you can sense that the other person is feeling a very strong emotion and needs a lot of reassurance and support.

Here are four Worksheets to help you.

WORKSHEET 1

Conversation between Friends

Here is a fragment of conversation between two very close friends. Read it through once or twice till you begin to get the feeling of how Kitty is handling her end of a very difficult situation. Then tackle the questions at the end of this worksheet.

K1   *Kitty:* Look—is there something on your mind today? You don't seem to be your usual self.

N1   *Norma:* Oh, is it as noticeable as that? I'm sorry, Kitty.

K2 *Kitty:* Do you feel like talking about it?

N2 *Norma:* Well, that might help, I suppose. (pause) Do you know, I hardly know where to start ... It's just that life's been so good for us recently ... Sue getting married, Pete having promotion at work, while I've been enjoying my spells of duty down at the C.A.B. office, but now ... Oh Kitty ... sorry ... (tears roll down her face, and she sobs for a while).

(Kitty puts her arm round Norma's shoulder and waits. Norma's sobbing grows quieter as she struggles to regain control.)

N3 *Norma:* Oh Kitty, (tears begin to roll down her cheeks again) I've found a lump on my breast!

(Kitty continues to hold Norma till the sobs subside and she gives a huge sigh.)

K3 *Kitty:* You've found a lump on your breast, Norma, and you're worried sick in case it's malignant.

N4 *Norma:* (her voice wavering) Yes—and I can't bear to tell Pete and spoil his happiness—after all, it may be quite harmless.

K4 *Kitty:* You don't want to give Pete all this worry in case there's nothing to worry about.

N5 *Norma:* (Nods, without speaking.) And I haven't the courage to go to the doctor without telling Pete first. He'd be hurt.

K5 *Kitty:* So you're cornered, and you're bottling it all up inside.

N6 *Norma:* Well, I'm letting it all out with you now. I suppose it's good that I've told someone. It's a bit of a relief, but I'm still worried. I wish I could remember where it was I read an article about lumps on the breast. It wasn't very long ago, but I can't find it. It gave some statistics about percentages that turned out to be harmless. Did you read that article?

K6 *Kitty:* Well, I have read some articles about it, but I don't know which one you mean. Norma, I think you want me to reassure you that everything will be all right, but it frightens me too.

N7 *Norma:* Yes, I am scared . . . but I might be making all this fuss about nothing.

K7 *Kitty:* You aren't sure about it.

N8 *Norma:* Yes—I'll *have* to see the doctor.

K8 *Kitty:* What I *do* remember reading is that, even if it is malignant, there are good chances of a complete cure nowadays if they catch it early.

N9 *Norma:* (speaking very slowly) The cold, hard facts . . . and this time we're talking about *me. I've* got a lump on *my* breast.

K9 *Kitty:* You sound as if you're facing up to it now.

N10 *Norma:* Uh-huh. I think that as long as I kept it to myself I could believe it might go away—like a bad dream does . . . Kitty, will you wait for a moment while I phone for an appointment? I don't think Pete would want me to wait, even till I had time to tell him.

In reflective listening, the task of the listener is to listen to the words said by the other person, and to sense the feelings that lie behind the words. When the listener thinks it is appropriate, he or she will then reflect back to the speaker, the content and/or the feelings of the message received. If you are listening to a person you do not know well, it may take some time to be on the correct wavelength for picking feelings. If you are listening to someone you know well, it is likely that you will be sensitive to the emotions going on inside him or her. In the above conversation, it is obvious that Kitty knows Norma very well and so was able to tell her exactly what she was picking up at the feeling level.

An Exercise

For you to think through by yourself, or with others

(*For your convenience, each part of the conversation between friends has been given a letter and number (eg K6) for easy reference in discussion.*)

1. *Go right through the conversation, and make a note of each time Kitty uses reflective listening to respond to Norma. Having done this, check the answers with those set out on p. 124, to see if you have picked up the technique correctly.*
2. *Now go through the conversation and pick out the places where your spontaneous response would have been quite different from Kitty's.*
   a) *For each one where yours would have been different, ask yourself, or discuss with others, the effect your remark might have had on the course of the conversation.*
   b) *Having thought it through, would you rather still use the response that would come spontaneously to you, or do you see any value in learning to respond with reflective listening?*

In Teaching

When I have used the above conversation in teaching, people have often said to me, 'The place in that conversation that I would have said something different would have been at K3. I know I would have said right away, "Have you been to the doctor?"' That always leads to a discussion on whether it is better for a friend to hand out advice or to support the other until she makes up her own mind what to do. What do you think? A friend might have listened very well before she gives advice but giving advice is not reflective listening. The temptation for most people who listen to others in distress is to hand out advice and reassurance. But people in distress are in the place where feelings preoccupy them. They are not where rational thoughts rule. It is uncomfortable, sometimes even frightening, to be with people who are in the grip of very intense unpleasant feelings. The instinctive reaction in most of us is to protect ourselves against being infected by what is upsetting others. Because of this we tend either to run away or consciously avoid being with upset people, or to make some attempt to command the unpleasant feelings to stop!

Have you ever heard yourself or others saying, 'Come on, now! You're losing grip of yourself!' 'Dry up those tears.' 'Put a brave face on it for my sake!' 'X would never have wanted you to carry on like this when he had gone' or 'But there's nothing to feel guilty about! You did what you could.' 'Feeling guilty won't get you anywhere.' 'You're upsetting Gran the way you're going on' or even 'A Christian has no right to feel like that!' As a result of remarks like these, mourners can sometimes feel rejected, unsupported, and completely misunderstood, on top of all their feelings of depression, anger, guilt or fear. Reflective listening gives permission to feel painful feelings. And grief is very painful. Those who do not allow themselves to feel the pain cannot work healthily through their grief. One of the main tasks of mourning is to feel the intense pain of the loss. Feeling supported and understood in the midst of the pain can make it bearable.

But reflective listening is costly. It takes much longer than it does to give advice. It demands that, for a time, the listener puts aside his or her own feelings of fear, to identify with the

pain of another. It is little wonder that many people choose to
love themselves instead of their neighbours, and choose not to
listen.

Some people seem to do reflective listening very naturally;
with others it feels stilted and awkward until they grow used
to it and know the right tone of voice in which to reflect back
what they have heard. Once you discover how supportive it
can be for another, you will probably want to practise it, and
to use it in lots of different situations—even those where there
is no grief around.

Answers

> *Here are the answers to question 1 on page 122.*
> *The following are the reflective listening replies:*
> *K1 (reflecting what she has sensed Norma's behaviour)*
> *K3: K4: K5:*
> *K6 (second sentence.)*
> *K7: K9.*

> *Here is another worksheet on which you can practise reflective*
> *listening, by yourself, or with others.*

WORKSHEET 2

Read through this fragment of a conversation between
Dugald, an elderly man whose wife died three months ago,
and a church visitor.

If you were the church visitor, and wanted to give Dugald a
reflective listening response, which would you choose from
the possible replies set out below in A–F?

Dugald: At first, when she was taken, I didn't know where
to turn. You see, she'd spoiled me. She always had

my meal ready on the table for me; she cleaned the house and did all the washing and ironing. Now and then I'd go to the shops with her, to carry home a heavy bag—but all the rest of the time she did everything for me. I suppose we always thought I'd be gone first, because I'd had a bad time with my heart when I was young, and she was always so healthy.

Visitor: You didn't think you'd be left alone.

Dugald: I did not. You know, for weeks I more or less lived on tea and toast, because I could manage that, and anyway, I didn't feel like eating much. Then my sister came, and she got a shock, because I'd lost so much weight. She was very good. She showed me how to cook one or two things and how to work the washing-machine . . . but why am I going on about this? You know that's not been the worst of it. It's that she's not around anymore. We were together for fifty-three years and there doesn't seem to be much point in living without her around. To be quite honest with you, I wish He'd take me too.

Visitor: (Select from A to F below)

A. Now now, Dugald, pull yourself together. You mustn't say things like that!

B. There must be something I could do to help you. Would you like me to do some ironing, perhaps?

C. If that happened to me, I would join one of the local pensioners' clubs. You'd get plenty of company there, and it would take your mind off things.

D. Remember that our times are in His hands.

E. You feel ready to join her.

F. But Dugald, what about your children, and grand-children. For their sakes you must go on. They need you even more now that your wife's away. Think about them and you'll feel different soon.

The reflective listening response on that worksheet is E. The words used in E are not the only words that could possibly make up a reflective listening response to Dugald's, but none of the other responses A to F are reflective listening ones.

An Exercise

For you to think through by yourself, or with others
The words used in E might not feel right to you. In fact, for some people, they would be very frightening words. In using them, the visitor is acknowledging that Dugald feels he would like to die.

If you were Dugald's visitor, would you be able to accept the fact that he might be feeling like that? Would it be all right for you to let him know that you were understanding his feelings?

If you would hesitate to reflect this feeling back to Dugald, think of your reason for not wanting to do it, and if possible, share this with others.

If reflective listening brings you face to face with a fear you have not faced, it may be better for you not to use it in such a situation (in spite of the fact that using it may be helpful for the person to whom you are listening).

The sense of the pointlessness of life without the person or job lost, is one of the most common responses in grief. Only a tiny percentage of people act on these feelings and try to end their own lives. By far the majority of people in our culture have within themselves the will and the strength to go on living. One thing that greatly strengthens the will to live is the feeling of being understood and supported by at least one other person.

If a person is suicidal . . .

Do not assume that because someone expresses a feeling of having little desire to live that they are suicidal. But if you are aware that someone is extremely depressed and is thinking of suicide, reflective listening is not enough! Do not leave such a person alone for any length of time. Get medical help without delay.

Now another worksheet—for you to think through, then perhaps to share with others.

WORKSHEET 3

Annette is a woman in her thirties, whose husband is asking her to divorce him. He is already living with another woman. A supportive friend is visiting her.

Imagine that *you* are that friend.

Annette: While the children are around I can keep going much as I've always done but it's at night, after the children are in bed, that I feel it most.

Friend: It's especially bad for you then.

Annette: Yes. (sighs) Sometimes I feel so depressed . . . there seems no point in going into the future without Dave . . . (her voice fades away into silence)

Friend: (says nothing for a while) Sometimes when you feel low, you just want to give it all up.

Annette: (Nods, and slightly shrugs her shoulders) . . . but then, there's Trudy and Mark. I've had to try to tell them what's happening, and they don't understand . . . How could they? But I can sense that they're scared that I'll go too. They keep popping back in for something or other when they're out playing. They didn't do that before.

Friend: As if they're checking to see that you're still there.

Annette: Suddenly, they need me more than they have for years, because I'm all they've got. Apart from the days when *he* chooses to come back and play at being the great father again! (The tone of Annette's voice has grown sharp and high, and the words 'great father' have been pronounced with sarcastic emphasis. She has straightened her back, and clenched her fists. Her knuckles are showing white under their skin.)

What emotion is Annette feeling at this point?

What reflective listening response might you give to show that you are understanding what is going on inside her?

Friend:

When you have written your response, check to make sure that you have reflected back to Annette in your own words, either what you have heard her telling you, or the feeling that is dominant in her at this point.

If you have given her any advice, score out your reply, and try again!

You can put reflective listening responses in many different words. There is no magic formula. Here are a few samples of reflective listening responses to Annette's last piece of conversation.

Friend: 1. So he comes back every so often.
2. You resent the fact that he's not taking his full responsibility with the children.
3. You're feeling very angry with him.
4. You want the children to be secure with both of you again.
5. His visits annoy you.
6. You feel very upset when he comes.
7. You are sounding angry right now.
   . . . and so on.

Was your response something along those lines?

If it was like the first response, it would have allowed Annette to go on telling her story.

If it was more like responses 2–7, it would have given Annette permission to express how angry she felt in that situation, how resentful that she had been left with all the responsibility while he went off, free to do what he liked. If she had permission to share her feelings, she might even have begun to share how personally rejected she had felt by him, and how she had been feeling unlovable, inadequate, and unattractive since she had found out he had gone to live with another woman. A person in Annette's situation normally has so many conflicting emotions warring inside her that she needs a lot of understanding and support to begin to get in touch with them and then to work through them. If she has a friend with whom she can share freely without feeling judged, she may well discover that she has enough resources to cope, and to make a successful new life for herself and the children.

Here is a final worksheet, with a variety of situations and emotions for you to test your skills in reflective listening. If you can share this with others, compare their responses with your own, and discuss together which replies are the most appropriate in each situation.

For you to do by yourself, or with others

WORKSHEET 4

Instructions:

Read what the speaker has said, until you understand

a) what is the speaker's problem?
b) what are the emotions he or she has about it?

Then, in the space provided, write a possible reflective listening reply.

SITUATION ONE

Widower of 80:

> I like to sit in the garden when the weather is fine. I look at the roses, and feel she is here with me, admiring them. She loved these roses. Used to fill the house with them at this time of year.

Visitor:

SITUATION TWO

Mother whose nine year old son was killed in a road accident:

> It's been six weeks now. Everyone else is back to normal. My life will never be the same again. When the children come out of school and down the street, shouting to each other, I can hardly bear to listen.

Friend:

SITUATION THREE

Young father, the day after he has been told that his new baby is severely mentally handicapped:

> They must be trying to cover something up! We're both healthy, so how can it possibly 'just happen' that we have a child like that? Did someone damage his brain at the delivery? Did they leave her too long in labour? I'm going to get to the bottom of this if it's the last thing I do!

Minister:

CHAPTER NINETEEN

Comfort

*He comforts us in all our troubles, so that we in turn may be able
to comfort others in any trouble of theirs and to share with them
the consolation we ourselves receive from God.*

2 Corinthians 1 : 4 (New English Bible)

Faith can bring comfort

When my aunt discovered that I was writing this book, she
wrote to me:

'I don't know whether you have ever come across anyone
who has experienced a sense of deep joy on the death of a
loved one. I did when father died. It was as if the certainty
of the victory over death overwhelmed me and left me with
"joy and peace in believing".

'It may well have been connected with the knowledge
that father's sufferings, which had been very great towards
the end, were at an end. I don't know. All I knew was that
abiding sense of God-given joy which kept bubbling up
through the tears.'

Another friend wrote:

'My mother died within seven weeks of her 100th
birthday. For the last ten years of her life she had felt that
life was no longer worth living. The nursing home phoned
me to tell me she had passed away peacefully at 1.30 a.m.,
and I went back to sleep, rejoicing that at last, her wish had
been granted.

One hour later I woke to 'see' her arriving on the other side. The solitary figure, with her back to me, rose out of mist and was about to join a throng of family ... it was like watching a play ... The picture faded and I was left with the assurance that all was very well.'

Many people testify to experiences that have come in the midst of desolation and pain, of a 'peace that passes understanding'. Yet for others, no such comfort comes from God. In fact, for many faithful people, there are months, even years of feeling cut off from his comfort before it is found again.

Searching for Comfort

One man had had a very severe drink problem but fourteen years had passed since he had a conversion experience and had stopped drinking alcohol.

His wife contracted cancer and died within a short six weeks of the diagnosis. Intense loneliness overwhelmed him.

Many years later he told me about that time. 'It was either prayer or the bottle for me. I prayed and prayed and kept praying, and eventually I got control, but I had to keep praying. I still can't think of that time without the feelings coming back to me.' As he spoke, there were tears in his eyes. Fourteen years of life in Christ had given him no automatic exemption from the struggle. What they had given him, was the belief that the One he worshipped had first-hand experience of suffering.

The idea of a suffering God is nonsense to many until they are face to face with pain. 'As for us, we proclaim the crucified Christ, who is the power of God, and the wisdom of God. For what seems to be God's foolishness is wiser than human wisdom, and what seems to be God's weakness is stronger than human strength.' 1 Cor. 1 : 22–25. (GNB)

From the depths of the pain of grief, people desperately seek comfort—and do so in all sorts of ways, and from many differing sources.

One little girl whose father died in hospital was with her mother when the nurse handed over the pyjamas which had been removed from his body. She reached out and grabbed the pyjama jacket. Every night for six weeks she put it on and slept in it. She said it smelled of her father. It gave her comfort.

A very responsible woman who was left with three young children to bring up alone, felt desperate for comfort one day. In the supermarket for groceries, she bought a bottle of wine. After the children were in bed that night, she drank it, and for the first time since her bereavement, felt the pain go. She did not repeat the experience because she knew she would have been unable to care for her children had an emergency arisen.

The acute loneliness and utter desolation felt at some severe losses, can be understood only by one who has been through them. It is easy to feel great compassion for someone in such a situation, and to claim 'I know how you must feel'! Do not too glibly say 'God will comfort you as he comforted me.' Such false comfort is rightly rejected if the grieving person has no proof that it is true. But many have received comfort from those who have been through an experience similar to their own, and who are unwilling to listen on the phone, or to come round to visit when understanding is needed. Christ often uses people to be his Body in the world today. Just as his touch had healing power in the gospel stories, so he can use our touch to bring healing and comfort to grieving folk.

One morning while in Australia, I picked up my mail on my way to work and opened it in the carwash. One letter was from my sister-in-law in Scotland, breaking the news to me that my brother's suspected stomach ulcer was, in fact, cancer, and that he had no more than two years to live. I was stunned then, but the following day I received a phone call to tell me he had died! Never had I felt so alone and cut off from home and family, and my attempts to pray brought no comfort. Somehow I felt as if I were suspended in space, alienated and almost disembodied.

Some days later I went on a staff training event led by a clergyman skilled in group dynamics. Although I physically sat in the circle with my colleagues, again I had the odd sensation that my body was somehow floating around somewhere else. During the day I watched vaguely as the trainer confronted one colleague after another about his or her behaviour in the group, and I remember thinking 'I'll not be able to cope if he talks to me. I really don't know what's happening here.' But he left me alone.

The day wore on, and we finished with a ceremony of celebration in which balloons were blown up, and messages written on them from one participant to another. People began to go around, hugging each other goodbye. I felt enormously exhausted and cut off. Normally I would not have done anything that would have brought attention to myself in such a situation. I would simply have joined in with the rest, but I remember feeling, 'Oh, I'm so glad that's all over,' and, lying down on the carpet on which we had sat all day, I rested my head on a big orange balloon and closed my eyes.

I heard footsteps passing me at one point, and the trainer's voice saying gently, 'Jean, whose breast are you leaning on?' 'It must be Mum's,' I replied. And he left me, to go on saying goodbye to the others. 'Yes,' I thought sleepily, 'he's right. I need Mum. I wish she was here to comfort me,' but it felt good just to be resting and to be allowed to rest.

Suddenly I was aware of a funny noise in my ear. Somebody was writing on my balloon! But I felt so tired, that I made no attempt to see who was writing. It would be one of my friends who would surely understand how tired I was.

Eventually I realised that I must pull myself together and get ready to go. I sat up, and took a look at the fresh message on the balloon. It said, 'See you. Jim.' The name of my brother who had just died in Scotland, was Jim.

I broke down. I sobbed and sobbed. I couldn't control myself. I was confused. Later I realised that the message was written by one of my colleagues, whose name also was Jim, but at that point I thought that somehow, someone was trying to comfort me by saying something on my brother's behalf!

Looking back, I am certain that one of my colleagues must have told the trainer about my recent bereavement or he would have confronted me about my non-involvement in the training group. At the point where I began to sob, he simply sat on the floor beside me, and held me against his own ample breast. Normally, I find it difficult to allow myself to cry in public— except for a quiet tear trickling down my cheek, but that day, while I was held, the sobs that came were so big and noisy that I felt sore.

Through my sobs I heard someone say quietly to the man who held me, 'Alan, don't you need to go?' I was conscious of him gently shaking his head as he held me securely while I finished weeping. I suspect I kept him late for his next appoint- ment. I don't know. All I know is that he held me until I was ready to be on my own again. I badly needed that catharsis of weeping, with a strong parent-figure holding me. I don't remember that he said anything to me. I did not see him after that day. I had no need to see him again. I was back in touch with reality.

Searching for what has been lost

One very common reaction to loss, is to search for the lost person or object. This is an obvious way to find comfort, if what is lost can be found, but many people engage in some kind of search after the death of someone meaningful to them. There are countless records of mourners attending spiritualist meetings and seances in the hope of getting back in touch with their lost loved one. Some seem to find comfort in this: others are disappointed or even deeply disturbed by the experience.

Those who talk with the bereaved will know how common

is the experience of one elderly widower who confided to a visitor, 'I'm so restless. I can't seem to sit still. I go wandering from room to room, and out into the garden. It's almost as if I expect to find her somewhere.' Others find themselves haunting places where they previously went with their dead partner, trying to capture some sense of their presence there.

These searchings are likely to stop during the regressive phase of grief. After that, going back to a place enjoyed together before a bereavement will be to bring back happy memories—not to look for the loved one. Some will visit a child's grave daily, tending it as if by doing so, they were caring for a living baby. The feeling that they can still do something for their child, gives a false sense of comfort for a while. And very similar to this are situations where those left behind keep a room exactly as it was before the death of the one who used it. Both are forms of denial: ways in which survivors try to get comfort in their pain by pretending that a death has not occurred. These are not healthy ways for comfort to be sought.

I have a very limited experience of people who have tried to get in touch with loved ones using Spiritualism. From what I have seen, I venture to suggest that those who are most certain that they have been in touch with dead relatives or friends, are likely to use this too, as a form of denial. Since they feel they can be in touch again with the person they have lost, there can be little incentive to readjust to life without him or her.

If you find someone behaving in these ways over a long period of time, it is an indication that he or she is stuck in the grieving process and may need professional help to move on.

Idealising the lost Person

For the first few weeks, and maybe months, after the loss of someone close to them, most mourners find their thoughts constantly centring around that person. Very often the

memories they replay time and again are the good ones, idealis-
ing the lost person.

Judy and Patty were neighbours. Often they would chat
while hanging out the washing. Judy would offer, 'Did you
hear what was happening yesterday? Really, sometimes I'm at
my wits end to know what to do to get Ron moving! He sits
there, engrossed in the paper, when the lawn is looking like a
hayfield! . . .' Patty would hear her out, making sympathetic
clucking noises every now and then, waiting till Judy paused
for breath. Then she would seize the opportunity to cap Judy's
tale with, 'Well, let me tell you about David on Sunday . . .'

Ron died very suddenly. The conversations over the back
fence between the two women were still initiated by Judy,
with thoughts centred round Ron, but after the funeral they
began to sound like this. 'You know, Ron was such a wonderful
husband. He never spoke a cross word to me. He would move
heaven and earth to get me whatever I wanted!'

Patty might well have countered, 'What? But Judy, don't
you remember telling me that . . .' or 'But we used to listen to
you two fighting every Sunday afternoon!' Patty didn't do
that. She listened. She didn't talk about David. She understood
that her neighbour was feeling very low, and that somehow
when she told stories which idealised her dead husband it was
an attempt to bolster up her flagging self-esteem. If he had
been a wonderful husband, then she could have been a wonderful wife—and she needed such reassurance to comfort her.

In fact, it was about eighteen months later before Judy said
to Patty, 'I was over visiting my daughter and her husband
yesterday, and do you know, it reminded me so much of me
and Ron! What a struggle she has to get him to do things! I
had quite a laugh to myself when I got back home!' Judy no
longer needed to remember Ron as perfect. Judy was adjusting
to life without him.

The passing of time usually lessens the intensity of the pain
of acute grief, but the mere passing of time in itself does not
always bring the true comfort of healing and readjustment.

Sometimes it brings instead a mute agreement to settle for a second best dulling of the pain rather than healing and new life.

In the next chapter we shall have a closer look at the alternatives to settling for living with accepted misery.

An Exercise

   For you to think through by yourself, or with others
   Examples of several ways of searching for comfort were mentioned in this chapter. Have you had similar experiences to these?
   For instance,
      can you remember going through a time of idealising something or somebody you had lost?
      can you remember a time when you felt you were searching for something or somebody you had lost?
      can you recall wanting to hang on to objects or surroundings in an attempt to believe you could still keep things as they were before your loss?
   If you can share such memories with others, take time to do so.

CHAPTER TWENTY

Grimly hanging on

When Mrs Brown's husband died, she was an active woman of sixty-five. They had been a very close couple, but had done a lot together for other people. Mrs Neil, a church visitor, had been calling on her every six weeks during the eighteen months since her bereavement. Each time she visited, Mrs Neil felt sure that, by the next time, Mrs Brown would be making some effort to face life again.

Mrs Brown: Oh, it's you. Come in.

Mrs Neil: And how are you now, Mrs Brown?

Mrs Brown: Oh, you know how it is, with all my aches and pains, I just don't get about the way I used to ... of course, no one wants to know you once you are a widow.

Mrs Neil: (very sympathetically) Oh dear, things don't sound too good for you.

Mrs Brown: Well, all I can say is, that if it ever happens to you, you'll know all about it! No one knows what it's really like until it happens to them. No one bothers with me any more. They're all too busy with their own pursuits. It was different at first, of course. People made a great fuss. They all came ... but now, everyone has forgotten me. (she gives a great sigh)

Mrs Neil: But, I'm sure some people must care about you! What about that new young neighbour you mentioned the last time I was here? Doesn't she call round sometimes to see if you want some shopping?

Mrs Brown: Oh her? She hasn't been back since she got a part-time job, so she was probably just filling in her time coming over to see me!

Later that day, Mrs Neil was sharing the evening meal with her husband.

Mrs Neil: Really, Tom, if I didn't feel it was my duty to go back and see her regularly, I can tell you that I'd never want to knock on her door again. I've had such a headache since I heard her complaining again! I don't know how long I can put up with it!

Mr Neil: My dear, it's getting to the stage when it's not only you who has to 'put up with it' when you do that visit. What about me? Can you not suggest that someone else takes that visit or tell her to pull herself together? I'm fed up with your moaning. Let's change the subject!

An Exercise

For you to think through by yourself, or with others

1. If you had been Mrs Neil, how would you have been feeling during the conversation with Mrs Brown?
2. Why do you think people have stopped coming around Mrs Brown?
3. Can you spot one way in which Mrs Neil is very like Mrs Brown?
4. If you were Mrs Neil, what would you do about Mrs Brown after that exchange with your husband?

Grief brings in its wake some very miserable feelings. But sometimes a grieving person grows so used to the misery and to coping with it, that it seems just too great a task to decide to get rid of it and to risk stepping out into life again. Mrs Brown had grown so used to receiving sympathy and to feeling sorry for herself, that she had not attempted to change in spite of the fact that fewer and fewer people were responding to her moans. Instead of making an attempt to help herself, she chose to put all the blame for her misery on others, so she could feel justified in playing the martyr. And it almost seems as if Mrs Neil had caught an infectious feeling from her! Feelings that are nursed for too long, produce behaviour which invites others to have bad feelings too.

Feelings arise in a 'here and now' situation. Something happens, and as a result we feel angry, or guilty, or happy, or sad, and so on. Along with these feelings comes energy to deal with that situation. If we suffer a loss, then we feel sad. A constructive way to deal with sadness, can be to weep. Weeping can relax muscles, take away some tension, and prepare us for beginning to make a new life without the person or thing we have lost. Along with anger, comes energy to fight, or to shout, or energy to put things right again. Along with guilt can come the motivation to ask for forgiveness or to work at making good the damage we have caused.

Here is a diagram to illustrate this:

	feeling + energy	expressing the	new situation
Situation >	to deal with >	feeling + dealing >	+ new feeling
	the situation	with the situation	+ new energy

If the energy is not used constructively, for expressing feeling and dealing with the situation, then things can go wrong. We can save up the feeling and its energy, instead of using it to deal with the situation. Sometimes people can condemn themselves to saving up a bad feeling for the rest of their lives. This is a bit like keeping a part of your body continuously septic, instead of getting rid of the poison, so that you can feel completely healthy.

After a major loss, there are so many feelings to be dealt with, and so many very sore and tender areas, that it does take most people a long long time to have the courage to look at, and then to deal with all the saved-up feelings. It is not wise to insist that people give up such feelings, until they are ready to do without them.

Anger, guilt and self-pity are three of the most common feelings found in grieving people. They are all feelings that others can understand, and for which they can offer genuine support for a reasonable period. But after that 'reasonable period' (and this will vary from person to person), sympathy can run out! A supportive person can sit for hours with a grieving friend who is hanging on to such a feeling long after it should have been dealt with. The friend can offer reflective listening, and more reflective listening, but there comes a point when the friend says, 'I've had enough! I'm feeling angry/depressed/ helpless/ guilty that I can't seem to get you to use the energy that comes with your feeling, to make things better for yourself.'

The grieving person has moved from being hurt by the loss to hanging on to the hurt, and so blocking the healing that otherwise could come.

An Exercise

For you to think through by yourself, or with others

1. Do you know anyone who has reached that stage at the moment?

2. If you do, how much do you care about that person . . .

>   *enough to do nothing,*
>   *and let him/her go on hurting self and others?*
>   *or*
>   *enough to risk*
>   *offering him or her information about what you can see happening?*

3. If you care enough to risk offering some information, jot down what the consequences of your confrontation might be: a) if it goes wrong . . .

   b) if it succeeds . . .

4. *If you have decided to do it, think through very carefully, what you might do and say. Do not blame the grieving person. Instead, point out what is happening and how you feel about it.*

5. *If you feel it would help, talk over your course of action with a wise friend, before you do it.*

6. *Pray for the person you plan to confront, and ask for wisdom for yourself as you do the confronting.*

7. *Be prepared to follow up your confrontation with reflective listening so that the grieving person feels understood and supported, and does not feel under attack.*

Here is an extract from the visit Mrs Neil paid to Mrs Brown six weeks after the one at the beginning of this chapter.

Mrs Brown: Oh it's you at long last. I thought you'd probably stopped coming, just like everyone else. Come in.

Mrs Neil: It's six weeks since I called, Mrs Brown. Just the same as usual. It sounds as if you've been feeling time dragging for you.

Mrs Brown: Time? That's all I've got since I lost my husband. When I think of all we did for others! We hardly had any time for ourselves. I'm just glad he's not here to know that no one cares about me, now. It would have broken his heart.

Mrs Neil: Mrs Brown, I don't think this is going to be easy for me, or for you, but I need to say something to you.

Mrs Brown: What do you mean?

Mrs Neil: It's just that I think I know why most people have stopped visiting you. Each time I have been to visit you recently, you have complained, and been so full of self-pity, that I haven't enjoyed your company. Other people might be feeling the same.

Mrs Brown: Oh . . . how could you say that! (bursts into tears) . . . Once it happens to you, you'll understand . . . (more tears)

Meanwhile, Mrs Neil sat in silence. She did not go over to comfort Mrs Brown as she used to, months ago, when she cried in her sadness. These tears were tears of self-pity, and she didn't want to reinforce them. So she waited—wishing she were anywhere but with Mrs Brown in that situation.

Mrs Brown: (sniffs, and gives Mrs Neil a reproachful glare)
Mrs Neil: I think you might be feeling angry with me for telling you all that, Mrs Brown, but I want you to have people calling again and enjoying their visits to you as much as they did in the old days. You were always so welcoming, and such good company. Do you remember when you gave a surprise tea-party for old Mrs Ferguson when she turned 90?
Mrs Brown: Yes, I remember . . . (sighs, and then gives a watery smile) You know, I think you're right. I was really hurt when you said what you did, but . . . maybe it's true . . . and maybe it's time . . .

The reality behind such a situation, is that people like Mrs Brown are often quite unaware of how their behaviour can be affecting others. It can come as a complete shock to them to be told how others are interpreting their actions. Those who had stopped coming to visit her, did so, because they imagined she was reacting as she was, quite deliberately and consciously.

In fact, it is just possible that you, too, are unaware that you are hanging grimly on to feelings you should have dealt with long ago! To give you some first-hand understanding of this, let these questions confront you, as you work through them.

An Exercise

For you to think through by yourself, and then, perhaps, to share with others

1. *Think of a significant loss you have been through. (Do not choose one that you have had in the past few weeks.)*
2. *When you recall that loss, what emotion do you feel most strongly?*
3. *What are you doing with this feeling? Are you hanging grimly on to it, and making yourself and others miserable when you do this, or are you using it to help you recover from the loss and adjust to a new life?*
4. *If you are grimly hanging on to that feeling, ask yourself— 'Why am I doing this to myself? What miserable thing am I getting out of it?'*

and then

    'Is this what I want, or do I want to readjust?'

5. *If you do want to readjust, ask yourself, 'What can I do to stop having this feeling?'*

and

    'Is this something I can stop by myself, with God's help, or do I need to talk it over with someone else?'

6. *Finally, outline your plan of campaign to get rid of the bad feeling.*

CHAPTER TWENTY-ONE

Dealing with guilt

Being able to say sorry, is, for most people, a way of keeping close relationships healthy. Because we are sinful
human beings, many of us put off keeping our relationships in
good order, thinking, 'I'll clear it up with her tomorrow' or
'There'll be time to explain what I meant the next time we
meet.'

One of the most difficult feelings to cope with in grief
is the impossibility of saying sorry to the person who has
died and of being offered forgiveness by him or her. We
have no way of making the relationship whole again and we
desperately want to do that before we feel emotionally able
to let them go. Often those left behind feel in some way
responsible for the death. 'I should have insisted that he see
the doctor months ago.' 'I was so caught up in my own
affairs that I didn't even think she might be needing me.'
'If only we hadn't had that argument before he went to
work!'

People have no way of coping with such harrowing remorse. Their normal method of saying sorry and making
amends is useless. Usually, as with any of the overwhelming
feelings experienced in the regressive phase, these lessen in
intensity as time slips by, but they are very easily brought
to the surface in the normal course of everyday living. While
such feelings are around, full recovery from grief is not possible. Friends tend to say, 'But you can't go on blaming
yourself like that! You'll make yourself ill. There's nothing
you can do about it, so put it out of your mind.' Sound
advice can be impossible to follow! People in the grip of

such emotions are not easily able to be as objective as that! Any help given to them, has to reach them at the feeling level—*where they are.*

Christian Resources

'You're feeling guilty? Well, then, the solution to that is very simple. You pray about it. You confess your sin to God. He forgives you. And that's that!' Can you hear a good, earnest Christian friend of yours giving out that advice? I can.

There are two major problems with that advice. The first is, that the grieving person will probably feel that the unfinished business is not with God, but rather, with the one they have lost through death. The mourner wants to ask his or her forgiveness, not God's. There are other ways to help with this, than by prayer.

The second problem about praying for forgiveness in that situation, is that the person who prays does not always *feel* forgiven. We can take a verse like 1 John 1:9: 'If we confess our sins to God . . . he will forgive us our sins and purify us from all wrongdoing.' Many have accepted that truth, and have felt forgiven. But others respond with 'I know I should be able to believe that I am forgiven because God's Word says so. I wish I could, but I don't feel forgiven.'

It doesn't really help to follow that up with, 'Well, whether or not you *feel* forgiven, you *are*, and you just have to believe it!' Such a remark could lead to the grieving person feeling even more guilty than before because he now feels that he is sinning against God. Alternatively, it could result in him saying to himself. 'This person just doesn't understand me. I'll get no further help here. I'll not mention it again.'

Symbols

Sometimes feelings respond wonderfully to the use of symbols. The mystery of the effectiveness of the sacraments 'ties in' here. Somehow, being handed and receiving the bread and wine, symbols of the suffering of Jesus for us, can make the breakthrough to feelings. If this sacrament is used to help a person receive the forgiveness of God for this kind of guilt, I believe that it greatly helps if the person receiving it is addressed by name: 'Mary, this is the Body of Christ, broken for you. Take it, and eat it to make you whole again.' 'Keith, this is the blood of Christ, shed so that your sins can be forgiven. Drink it, and remember him.'

In the prayer with the sacrament, it helps if the specific guilt the person is feeling is put into words, if possible, by the grieving person. If this is not suitable, then it can be done on his or her behalf by another. Now that more and more Christian people are gathering together in house-groups, these can be ideal settings, both for the sharing of feelings when someone needs help and support, and for offering healing through prayer and sacrament.

There is another symbolic act that can be most effective in helping a person feel forgiven. After the grieving person has shared with a housegroup, or even with a caring friend, such feelings of guilt and remorse, invite him or her to write on a piece of paper what it is they want to be forgiven. (If this is done in a housegroup, everyone may want to join in and write things for themselves.) Fetch matches, and a container in which it will be safe for paper to burn (e.g. an ashtray). Read together a verse like 1 John 1:9 or Psalm 103:12. Burn the piece of paper until only the ash remains. Then have a short prayer of thanks for forgiveness, and of rededication of the life made clean and whole again. And if, at the prayer of dedication, loving hands are laid on the head and shoulders of the one who has received forgiveness, this will also help that person feel loved and forgiven again.

Other Resources to use

Ruth worked in a down-town team ministry. As she climbed the stairs of an old tenement property, she gave a sigh. 'If only he could forgive himself, Lord!' In her mind's eye she could see old Sandy as she had left him at the previous week's visit. His eyes had been dull and listless. What a contrast to the cheery little man who had always had a joke on his lips, and who had managed so capably to look after his wife until her fatal attack a month ago!

The only time Ruth had glimpsed a spark of his old energy was when he had responded to her sharing of a specially happy visit she had paid to his wife, Molly, a few months before. Almost immediately he had begun yet again to tell her how he had gone out to his pensioners' club that afternoon, leaving a neighbour with his dear wife, and of how another neighbour had had to fetch him from there. Molly had been dead before he could make it home to her. 'I went out to enjoy myself,' he had muttered, 'just when she needed me. Selfish, through and through, that's me. *She* couldn't get out. Why did *I* want to? I'll never forgive myself.' In response to this, Ruth had attempted to reassure him that she knew no one as faithful and attentive as he had been to Molly these past years since her first stroke. He had seemed not to hear her at first, then had whispered, 'But when she really needed me, I wasn't there.'

Sandy's door was in front of Ruth again. She knocked. When he came, he smiled. 'Come away in,' he said. 'She always looked forward to your visits.' He seemed to be looking a bit better than he had done the previous week. Ruth was aware of the smell of furniture polish in the living room. She commented on the shine on the old dresser, and he smiled a bit. 'I thought to myself this morning, that she wouldn't have wanted to see the place so dusty. So I set to work, and when I sat down with a cup of tea afterwards, I fancied I could hear her saying, "Sandy, you've done a good job!" ' But almost immediately his expression changed, and his voice lowered. 'It meant so much for us to be together, in our own home . . . We never wearied. I'll never forgive myself for leaving her that day— when she needed me . . .' and his voice tailed off to a whisper.

Ruth waited a moment, and then very gently said, 'Sandy, may I ask you to do something which might help?'

Without looking up, he said, 'Aye . . . I can't get it out of my mind.'

'Sandy, will you imagine that Molly is sitting in her chair over there again?'

'I do that often,' came the reply.

'Right then,' continued Ruth. 'Speak to her, just as you used to, and tell her how you've been feeling about going out that day.'

'Molly, lass,' he began, and tears started to trickle down his face. He swallowed. 'Molly . . . I went off and left you . . . I didn't know you were so near the end . . . I should never have gone, lass.'

Very gently, Ruth prompted, 'Sandy, do you want to say sorry?'

There was silence in the room, while the muscles of Sandy's mouth worked to regain control. 'I'm sorry, lass,' he mumbled.

Ruth went on, 'Look at Molly, and listen to see if she has something to say to you now.'

She watched as Sandy raised his head to look again in the direction of the big easy chair. She waited. His shoulders began to heave. He fumbled for his handkerchief. He wept.

After a while, Ruth went over and laid a comforting hand on his shoulder. Gradually, the sobbing ceased, and he blew his nose. 'I'm fine now. Can I tell you what she said to me?'

'I'd like that,' Ruth replied.

'She just said, "I love you, Sandy" and then she said, "Be good to yourself, now. You deserve it." You know, that's what she always used to say to me.'

'And how are you going to be good to yourself, then?' asked Ruth, returning to sit on her chair.

'Well, the first thing I'm going to do is to stop kicking myself for going out that day. If I had known, I wouldn't have gone, and I'm sure she knows that.'

'And is there something else?' asked Ruth.

'It'll be hard, but I need the company ... I think I'll be able to go back to the pensioners' club now.' He looked up at Ruth to see her reaction. She smiled, with relief, as well as with love for him. 'Sandy, that's great! I feel sure that's exactly what Molly would have wanted you to say!'

Gestalt

Ruth had used a technique she had learned in a class on Gestalt therapy when she invited Sandy to talk with Molly as if she were present in the room. Each person carries with him or her, a unique perception of the significant figures with whom he or she has related all through life. These are rather like a library of video recordings which can be replayed at will. Feeling quite certain that Sandy would have a strong positive memory of how Molly would have reacted in that situation, had she still been alive and well, Ruth felt confident in enabling him to get in touch with this. Had she sensed that he would hear blaming criticism come from his memory of Molly, she would not have used this technique.

In his insecurity after the shock of Molly's death, Sandy had cut himself off from this source of comfort and was only allowing himself to play a series of old tapes in which he had been blamed for being selfish. Most of us have quite a stock of these! The technique Ruth used, unblocked the flow of nurturing energy he had stored up from his relationship with Molly over the years.

It is difficult for us to do this for ourselves. It is best done with a loving parent-figure who will temporarily look after us until we can tap again into our own resources for parenting ourselves.

There is no room to say more here about such techniques, except to recommend counselling courses to caring people. The skills taught can be extremely useful in ministry.

Had Ruth had no formal training in counselling, she could, in this situation, simply have asked a straightforward question like, 'What do you think Molly would say to you if she were here listening to you now?'

That question may not be quite as effective as Ruth's counselling technique because it is not quite so likely to get right through to the guilty feeling. But it sometimes works beautifully and is well worth trying if you do not feel you can work like Ruth.

Here is a word of advice however, 'Don't say, "I'm certain that if Molly was here, she would say to you . . ."' These words come from *your* image of Molly which may be quite different to Sandy's image. It's Sandy's memory that has to look after him—and he can't have you with him always anyway.

Guilt

In the previous chapter it was mentioned that people often hang on to guilt for a long long time. Usually, when a person does this, there is a need—perhaps a subconscious need—for that person to pay for the guilt by punishing him or herself. Somehow or other, there is the belief that this is the only way to make up for what was done—or left undone.

Margo lost her oldest child as a result of an accident. She had sent him off on his bicycle to post a letter for her during the evening rush-hour traffic. She could easily have waited till later that evening when the roads would have been quiet again. But by that time, her son had been killed.

Without fully realising what she was doing, Margo allowed herself to dwell so much on her guilt for the accident, that she seriously damaged the relationship she had with both her younger children. Eventually, her youngest was caught stealing a bicycle, and Margo had to attend several sessions of counselling at the Child Guidance Clinic with him. It was there she was confronted with the results of the guilt she had hung on to for years. With the help of the psychologist she began to relate better to her remaining children. But Margo had many friends who could lovingly have shown her what they could see was happening, long before the crisis in the family. They hadn't liked to 'interfere'.

If you encounter someone in this position, the loving thing to do could be to confront him or her with what you see is happening. When you have given that person accurate data that you have observed, then you can ask something like: 'Why are you doing this to yourself and your children?'

If the one you are supporting can then realise that, in some way, it seems as if she is punishing herself, you can go on from there. But if you get a reply that conveys that she has not understood you, you may wish to be more direct and say words to this effect: 'It seems to me that you may be punishing yourself still for what happened four years ago—and not only yourself, Margo, but you are making your children pay for it, too.'

If the person can sense that you care and can feel that this diagnosis of the situation might be correct, you could follow up with a confronting question like: 'How many more years do you have to suffer for this, and make others suffer? When will your guilt be paid for?' This can be the loving confrontation that stops the guilt spreading its poison from year to year, from relationship to relationship. The person will realise that there is something she can do to make the situation better, and, perhaps with your support, she will figure out what this can be and put it into action.

Remember that it is possible for a person to go on, from day to day, week to week, even year to year without being fully aware of what is happening in present relationships because of damage done in the past.

Some Guilt requires Professional Help

If you think somebody you know needs more help with guilt than you can give or than is available through the church, do encourage him or her to go to the doctor for further help.

An Exercise

For you to think through by yourself, or to discuss with others

1. *Have you ever had the experience of feeling very guilty after a loss? If so, why did you feel guilty, and how did you deal with your guilt?*

    If you suspect that you have not yet fully dealt with it, where could you go to get the forgiveness you need?

2. *If you are using this book in a group, discuss with each other what help you could offer to someone feeling guilt after a loss.*

    Begin by sharing your reactions to the suggestions in this chapter.

CHAPTER TWENTY-TWO

Saying goodbye

Time does often heal. People adjust from life as it was to life as it has to be now. And each does so, in his or her own way.

A Progression of Goodbyes

Looking back over the five years since his wife's death, Nigel could see a series of incidents, each one of which had helped him readjust to life without her. Although her illness had been very short, they had both known she could not recover. They had time to say goodbye. Painful as it had been, they had talked together before her death, about the future. In so many ways, that sharing had eased his initial readjustment.

Then there had been the day he took all her clothing to the Oxfam shop, came home, opened the wardrobe, and cried till he could cry no more. One weekend he had spent re-reading all the letters sent to him on her death, then he had placed them in a shoebox, tied a ribbon around them and put them away in the attic.

The next hurdle had been the summer holiday. Bravely he had booked a coach tour. During most of it he had felt numb. It meant little to him without her company. On the last evening, there was a party where most of his fellow-passengers had too much to drink. One man, who, like himself, had seemed alone for most of the trip, cornered him. He had lost his wife ten years before, and full of maudlin self-pity, had poured out his story to Nigel. Nigel went through a whole gamut of emotions as he listened to the tale—pity, anger, compassion, revulsion, alarm, but it was that incident that helped him to say to himself, 'In ten years' time, I'm not going to be like that! As soon as I return from this holiday, I'll start getting into things again.'

He did. Two years later he had invited out a woman who had lost her husband around the time of his own loss. He began to consider remarriage. As it turned out, he did not marry the widow, but the fact of having to think about it was another milestone in his readjustment process. His daughter had reacted very negatively to discovering that her father had a woman friend, and it was as he reasoned with her that he realised two very important things. First, that she was right on one score. This woman was not a person who was likely to give him the kind of marriage in which he would feel happy and fulfilled. But, strong though his daughter's feelings were, she was wrong in claiming that he could never again find happiness in marriage. He could understand that it would be difficult for her to have him married to someone who was not her mother but that was not sufficient reason for him to remain single for the rest of his life.

Now, five years after his bereavement he was about to remarry and he was happier than he had thought he ever would be again. He was spending a last evening alone in the home he had shared with his wife and daughter. It had been sold and emptied, apart from what he required for that night. He wandered through the garden, and through each room in the house, reviving old memories, and letting them go. Then he sat quietly, thinking of all that his relationship with his wife had given to him. He remembered the difficulties in their relationship, the troubles they had worked through together, the corners they had rubbed off each other, and their times of joy and contentment.

Before he went off to sleep, he prayed. He thanked God for all that had been in the past, and he handed that over to Him. His goodbyes were completed.

Adjusting to a delayed Goodbye

Alan had risen quickly to being a junior manager in his firm. His future appeared to be financially secure. Then he was made redundant. His father-in-law had a small hardware business, and was due to retire within the next few years so he invited Alan to come into partnership with him. Although it was not what Alan would have chosen, he decided to join him. By the time his father-in-law had retired, Alan was working very hard, and the business was expanding. When she could, his wife, Catriona, helped out, but as she had two little children to look after, her availability was limited. Then Alan died.

Catriona's reaction to his death was to say immediately: 'I owe it to Alan and to my father to take Alan's place.' She brought someone in to look after the children, and, knowing she could have her father's advice, began to run the business. Rather than consult her father, she often thought: 'What would Alan have done?' and then carried that out.

Four years went by. Both her children were now at Primary School, and required to be looked after only for one hour in the morning and two in the late afternoon, before she arrived home. One evening one of her close friends came round for a chat.

'You're looking a bit tired, Catriona. Are things busy for you just now?'

'They're hectic. Two of the girls in the shop are off with 'flu, and I've had to serve at the counter. Most nights I have to bring the books home with me. It's a good break for me tonight with you here.'

'Catriona, why do you do it? Why do you keep on the shop? What do you get out of it? There must be lots of other things you could do which would be easier on you—and on the kids.'

'I don't know, really,' replied Catriona. 'I suppose I wouldn't like to see all Alan's hard work—and my father's, of course—go for nothing.'

'But, look, is it what *you* would choose to do, or is it what Alan felt *he* had to do?' her friend persisted.

That night and in the days after that conversation, Catriona began to think about her life. Within a year, she had sold the business, and been accepted as a mature student at a nearby Teacher Training College. She had begun to do what she wanted to do and to organise her life so that she would be able to be with her family more often.

Thanks to her friend's concern, she had come to realise that, by stepping into Alan's shoes, she had been able in some way to deny the reality of his death. She had not let him go, but had been trying to complete his life for him. As she sold the shop, she said goodbye to her need to keep him around.

A Goodbye which might have been overlooked

Maggie and Neil had been married in their late thirties. They both longed to have children, but it was over a year before Maggie became pregnant. The baby miscarried at three months, just before the time at which they had decided to share their good news with their families and friends. The doctor explained to Maggie that this kind of miscarriage was probably a sign that there had been some type of abnormality of the foetus and that she should be glad that it had aborted when it did. So Maggie tried to be glad and to go back to work as if nothing had happened.

Time went on, and Neil grew more and more concerned about Maggie. She wouldn't go to church on the Sundays she knew babies were to be baptised. She dropped all contact with a very close friend who had recently had a baby. Each month there were days when Maggie was likely to be tearful. 'Shouldn't you see the doctor?' Neil tried to reason. 'No. I don't need the doctor,' Maggie insisted. Eventually, Neil talked to their minister about it. 'Tell Maggie you have told me this and let me know what she says,' he advised.

When he told her, Maggie cried again, but decided she

needed to talk over how she was feeling with someone who would give them some support. And so the minister came to their home, and listened till he felt he understood that Maggie was mourning for the child she had carried inside her for three short months. He helped her to talk about how she felt when she knew she was carrying a child in her womb. And he asked Neil about his reponse, too.

'Had you decided on a name for your baby?' he asked gently.

The couple smiled at each other. 'We wanted to name him Andrew if he was a boy,' volunteered Maggie. 'So when we talked about him for those few weeks, we called him "Andy",' added Neil.

'So you had begun to say hello to Andy, and to feel how much he belonged to you both, when out of the blue, you were faced with his death,' explained the minister. Maggie's eyes filled with tears. Neil nodded and quietly added, 'That's how it felt.'

'When someone we love dies, we normally arrange a funeral service to help us say goodbye to them, and to formally hand them over to God's care. We can't give a funeral to Andy, but I'd like to help you do something similar for him.' Neil reached over and held Maggie's hand as the minister asked, 'May I do that?' They nodded.

'Just where you are,' the minister continued, 'sit back on the couch till you feel it supporting you, then close your eyes.' Maggie and Neil did as he suggested. 'Now will you imagine you are holding Andy in your hands. He's very tiny, but he's your little son. As you hold him, say something to him . . .' He waited, and watched the faces of the young couple. Tears were trickling down Maggie's cheeks. Neil's face was relaxed.

'You are not alone with Andy. Jesus has come to be with you all. He's looking down lovingly at your baby, too . . . Maggie, Neil, tell Jesus what you want to say to him about Andy . . .' He waited for a while, and then went on, 'And listen to what Jesus has to say to you about your baby . . .'

After about thirty seconds he said, 'Now, give Andrew to Jesus, just as you would if you had brought him to be baptised. Watch as Jesus receives him from you . . . and say goodbye to him.' He paused again.

'Maggie and Neil, it's time to leave little Andy with Jesus. Let Jesus give you both His blessing as you go. When you are ready, come back to the experience of being in your own living room again. And open your eyes.'

Almost immediately, Neil opened his eyes, smiled across at the minister, then looked at Maggie. Maggie took much longer to open her eyes, but as she did, she stretched out her hand to hold Neil's, then said quietly, 'That was beautiful, but it was hard to come away.'

'It was a good experience for you, then?' enquired the minister.

'Yes,' Maggie said. 'It was. Somehow, I feel quite different now. Before that, I thought it was somehow wrong for me to think of Andy as a real person, and as somebody who would matter to Jesus too. Now I know he does.'

'Did you feel that Jesus was saying anything to you in that experience?" asked the minister.

'Yes . . . He told me that He knew how I felt . . . and I said to Him, "But why did You give him to me, then take him away?" . . . He didn't give me an answer in words. He put his arm round my shoulder instead . . .'

"And how did you feel then?'

'Understood . . . as if He knew all about me . . . and as if He had everything under control . . . You know, after that, I was just going to hand my baby over to Him to keep for me when I heard your voice telling me to do it. Now I'm sure that Andy is with Jesus.'

The Minister bent over and put his hand on hers, as he said, 'And Neil, how was the experience for you?'

'Good,' replied Neil, 'but a bit different from Maggie's.'

'Tell us about it.'

'I couldn't say I really saw Jesus, or heard him speak . . .

but what happened to me was that suddenly I felt full of love for . . . (here he cleared his throat) . . . for Andy. You see, I think that before, when I was sad, I was sad for Maggie, and I was sad that I hadn't become a father . . . I don't know, but for me, Andy had been more an idea than a baby . . . Anyway, it was when you asked us to give the baby to Jesus that I felt His presence . . . I knew He was here. That was quite something!'

A Comment on that way of saying Goodbye

If you have neither experienced nor read of that way of praying with people, the illustration involving Maggie, Neil and the minister may seem a very strange one to you. The particular method used here is one which is often called 'the healing of the memories'. There are now a number of books written about this specifically Christian technique.* It appears to be, and indeed is, a simple way of enabling people to deal with the past and to see it in a new light. But please do not try to handle a situation like this until you have read a lot more about the theory behind it. It is best handled by people with counselling skills.

'The healing of the memories' always involves helping people to relax and then to imagine a scene into which they invite Jesus. The scene can be a well-remembered hurtful incident in the past. Or it can be, as it was here, a specially constructed incident that is totally in keeping with what the people experiencing it will find acceptable, and with what you, the enabler, feel will be helpful for them. I believe that when I lead a person into such an experience, that the Holy Spirit guides me—helps me to understand that person and gives me discernment as I direct them.

---

* I realise that many caring people who may read this book may not identify with the Christian faith, and often those who need help will have no personal faith in Christ. If the carer, or those being helped, believe in God, this technique could be used with His Name.

I keep a close and prayerful watch on what is happening as each person is undergoing the experience. I watch to see what that person's facial expressions and body movements are saying to me. If I feel out of touch with what is going on inside that person, then I say something like, 'Maggie, tell me what is happening,' and I respond to her reply, gently helping her through the experience.

There has to be a fair measure of trust between the enabler and the person who is receiving such help, and so I rarely do this kind of thing with a person I do not know very well. But the most important factor in this way of helping is the belief the person being helped has in Jesus.* If that person believes that He is One who can understand completely, and yet can go on loving him/her and each other person in the reconstructed incident, then the Spirit often uses this kind of approach to transform the attitude of the person having the experience. In it, the person begins to see others as he/she believes Jesus sees them.

This method can be helpful even in situations where the person experiencing it has been feeling out of touch with spiritual things. It can release him or her into a new relationship with the living Christ.

I was helped to say Goodbye

I find it difficult to begin to write about this particular personal experience, because, while it was happening to me I was so emotionally caught up in it, that it is hard to remember it in a logical fashion. I will try to reconstruct it.

Most of the other people on that House Church training week were people I had been getting to know through my work in the Church of Scotland. Dr Phil Anderson, a professor from Chicago Theological Seminary, was our trainer. Since studying under him in America, I had a great love and respect

---

* See footnote to p. 161.

for him. Phil led us through a wide variety of experiences in these few days.

Evaluating an exercise in which we had been working with a partner, I tried to put my feelings into words and found myself unable to do so because of tears. I was very upset. Something had triggered off the feelings I had had at the time of my mother's death, but which I had not allowed myself to face.

I had been in Australia when the news of her heart attack had been phoned through to me. I had been told that the attack was so severe that it would be likely to be followed by another and this one fatal. There was an overnight delay in my setting off for Scotland on the first plane I could book. Alone for an hour or two, I had paced back and forward in an empty house repeating over and over, 'Mum, wait for me. Wait till I get back. I'm coming. Wait for me.' But another phone call before my plane left told me she had not waited. I spent the two-day flight to her funeral curled up on plane seats, feeling nothing but a huge, empty ache. Mum had always been there, waiting for me when I needed her. I felt abandoned.

Back with the rest of my family, there was no room for such a disloyal, irrational feeling. But two and a half years after her death, it had now caught up with me, unbidden.

I do not now remember how Phil managed to persuade me to tell that group of people that feeling, because I was so ashamed of feeling it. It seemed utterly disloyal to my mother who had so loved and cared for me to accuse her of abandoning me, and to feel angry with her for not staying alive till I could say goodbye to her! She could not choose when to die! I wanted to reject my feelings. But eventually, Phil managed to have me picture my mother, and say aloud to her 'Mum, why did you not wait?' Then through all the jumble of my emotions, I heard him gently insist that I listen to what she would say to me. To my surprise, I felt that she was saying, 'I had to go. Jim needed me more than you did.'

Jim, my brother, her first-born, had died less than three months before her, and I knew that she couldn't have recovered from that by the time of her own death, but I had never given any conscious thought to that. What I felt she was saying to me, seemed completely reasonable at that moment. 'Of course! Why didn't I think of that? Of course she would want to comfort him after all the suffering and pain he had been through. He was her little boy.'

My anger and hurt at her had been expressed, but Phil had not finished with me. He urged me to tell Mum what I would have said had I reached home in time. And so I had the chance of telling her again how much I loved her and how much all her mothering had meant to me. I said goodbye and she was gone. I could no longer picture her there.

Phil then asked me to go round the group of people who had been watching as he helped me through this experience. One by one they hugged me and told me what it had meant to them to be there with me. Somehow, I had imagined that some of them would have wanted to reject me because I had been disloyal to my mother. But that had been my feeling, not theirs. Apparently there were some in the group who had been helped to do their own grieving as they watched me do mine.

For the rest of that day I felt utterly exhausted, and yet as if a huge black cloud had lifted from me. For two and a half years I had been unable to think or speak of my mother's death without feeling pain and wanting to cry. From that day to this there has been no more pain when I think of her. I still have times when I miss her and tears have come to my eyes, but I know I have said goodbye to her as far as my time on this earth is concerned. I no longer needed her to be here for me.

Owning forbidden Feelings

In helping others as Phil helped me then, I have noticed time and again that relief and release come when mourners are able to own feelings that, for some reason or other, were forbidden to them previously. I cannot imagine ever summoning up enough courage, had my mother still been alive, to accuse her, angrily, of abandoning me when I needed her. Anger was not part of our relationship. I know she was a very good mother to me: I believe that I needed to feel that she was a perfect one. How could I have let a perfect mother go?

For many other people, saying goodbye to parents has meant owning the fact that they loved them!

One minister I knew, whose father had been a minister before him, had a tremendous struggle to say goodbye to him. His father had been a hard-working, conscientious pastor for his flock, but a remote, demanding father to his son. He expressed his love through the demands he made on him. He rarely touched him, and it would have been unthinkable to his son to have heard, from his father, the words 'I love you.'

We got nowhere in the counselling relationship by helping Bob picture his father as he remembered him. His actual experience of his father blocked any possibility of a more relaxed and demonstrative interaction.

And so we talked together of our belief that his father was now in the presence of Jesus and would be changed by experiencing His love. Only then could the son begin to think differently of his father. He was able to believe that his father no longer needed to shield himself from receiving and expressing love, since the Holy Spirit would have completed the work he began to do in him while he was living in the world.

So, as I worked with Bob, there were two pictures of his father we could use. He could see his father as he had been and he could imagine him as he now is, in his new freedom. I invited him to relax, and to imagine that he was standing by his father's open grave, at his funeral. As the earth was thrown on top of the coffin, I asked Bob to say goodbye to his father as he knew him. He did that, and then something began to happen. As he watched, waves of energy seemed to be flowing from the newly filled grave! Bob was having a visual experience of what he believed had happened to the man whose worn-out body lay there.

(As his counsellor, I had no idea till he told me, later, of what he was visualising. I only knew by watching Bob's face, that all seemed well with him.)

I then asked him to meet his 'new-created' father and to say to him what he wanted to. Here is what he later wrote about that experience.

There he was, the renewed Dad—buried yet raised; the Dad he was created to be, the man re-born to that fullness of life which was his, yet seemed to have been hidden in his head, sought for in theological terms, in thinking the right things, in keeping feelings in their place.

This Dad put his arm around my shoulders, and I said to him, 'We've so much to talk about.' We then agreed to take our time, and that we'd meet again, and off we went with arms round each other's shoulders—those places of heavy burdens.

A few days after the counselling session Bob had two dreams. In one he had an argument with his father, but was left with no hurt about their difference of opinion. This was in complete contrast to his previous experience. In the second dream, his mother, father and he all had fun together—something Bob had no conscious memory of having experienced while they were alive. And a few days after that Bob was sitting alone, reading and thinking. Read about it in his words again: 'And suddenly, I thought of Dad, and said "I love you. I love you. I love you." And through my half-formed tears, it was good. I didn't see, but rather, felt, that all was well with him—that he knew, and felt and understood and didn't need me to change for he had changed and I had changed and neither of us said "I told you so". I felt a relationship and all was well, and all manner of things were well."

As I write, Bob's experience is very new. I believe that the Holy Spirit has worked in his life to help him say goodbye to the destructive part of the relationship he remembers having with his father. The healing love of Jesus is transforming the way Bob feels about himself. He is becoming the loving son of a loving father.

An Exercise

For you to think through by yourself, and then share with others

1. *Have you lost any person or thing in the past and not yet fully said goodbye?*

   Here are some points to look for as you answer that question

   a) *When you speak or think of that person or thing, do you still feel pain?*

   b) *Are you still hanging on to any emotions (e.g. resentment, guilt, an unfulfilled longing) that ought, by now, to be in the past?*

   c) *Are you still pretending in some way that your loss is not real?*

   d) *Are you unable to acknowledge both good and bad qualities in the person or thing you have lost?*

If your answers are 'yes', then you have probably not said goodbye.

2. *If you still have someone or something to let go, what will you need to do to say goodbye?*

   When will you feel ready to do this?

   Do you need help to do it?

   If so, what kind of help, and from whom?

3. *If you are supporting someone who has not yet said goodbye, what might you say or do to help that person let go of the need to hang on?*

CHAPTER TWENTY-THREE

Do you need apple pie?

'There's nothing to beat a slice of your apple pie, Sarah, m'dear,' Victor would say each time she served it. After Victor died, Sarah continued to bake apple pies. She gave them to friends and neighbours and church fetes, and if in return she was told how special they were, she glowed. Through her apple pies, Sarah looked for the appreciation she needed.

An Exercise

For you to think through by yourself

What do you need from a close relationship?
List all the things you can think of.

Having done that, read on.

Winston married a girl with very little self-confidence. He was strong and successful enough for both of them. Her diffidence had the effect of making him seem even more competent than he was. The marriage ended in divorce. It first began to show signs of strain after she joined a women's group. Friendships there encouraged her to believe in herself and she discovered gifts hidden behind her shaky self-esteem. Not only did she rise to leadership, but she was appointed to an international committee. Winston could not cope with a wife who had grown to look more competent than he.

Communication broke down between them. They separated.

Winston found another partner—a young woman, greatly lacking in self-confidence.

Symbiotic Relationships

Symbiosis is a word that means 'living together for mutual benefit'. If you are in a relationship with someone on whom you depend to supply some of your emotional needs, then you have a symbiotic relationship.

Most of us might interpret the phrase 'mutual benefit' as 'for the good of healthy, loving relationships'. In fact, what we get from such relationships is reinforcement to go on thinking of ourselves and the other involved as we have grown used to doing. And so Sarah 'needed'* a relationship where her skill was appreciated.

Winston 'needed' a relationship where he was seen to be competent because of the incompetence of the other. Winston's wife realised that she no longer 'needed' a relationship which reinforced her low self-esteem. Once she had support to discover that she was competent, she could step out of the symbiotic part of her relationship with Winston. But when she did that, she was no longer giving Winston what he 'needed'! The 'mutual benefit' had gone.

Look back to the list you wrote, near the beginning of this chapter, of your needs in a close relationship.

Did you make a list of positive things like love, trust, security, encouragement, loving touch, sharing of interests, and so on? Most seem to appreciate these in a healthy, loving relationship.

Human beings are odd creatures! Instead of acting as if these were all we needed, we often act as if we wanted very different things from close relationships. In fact, it is normal

---

* 'needed' is in quotation marks because it is used in an unusual way. 'Needs' like these can be changed!

for people like us to want to have times when we are not too close! To achieve this:

we act as if we need some to fight with,

> someone to blame, or to blame us,
>
> someone to manipulate, or to manipulate us,
>
> someone to put down, or to be put down by,
>
> someone to withdraw from, or make us withdraw,
>
> someone to hate, or be hated by . . . and so on.

Symbiosis in Childhood can influence grown-up Relationships

Craig had a very dominant mother. She felt she knew best what was right for Craig, and continually told him so. She used to play a nasty game with him in which she would say, 'I wish you would learn to make up your own mind? Go and think about it!' When Craig came back, having thought about it, she would pull his reasoning to bits with sarcastic comments, inform him that he still had not learned to make up his own mind, and then tell him what he ought to have thought. Since Craig was quite a bright boy, he quickly assumed that there was little point in thinking things through for himself when his mother was around. At school he learned to make decisions about the work he was assigned, and, encouraged by his teachers, he did well.

Craig was quite content to marry a woman who took complete responsibility for all decisions about their home and family life, while, in the business world, he was quietly competent in decision-making. Initially, his wife had wanted him to discuss things with her and to arrive at shared decisions, but he had shown such resistance, that she resigned herself to fitting in with what he seemed to want. Occasionally, when she became irritated with him, she said, 'Craig. It beats me how you manage to cope at work if you refuse to take decisions!' To such remarks, Craig gave no answer. The symbiosis they had developed met his needs, and she was willing, and able, to play it his way.

An Exercise

For you to think through by yourself

Think of a close relationship you have at the moment.
What does that person reinforce for you about the beliefs you have about yourself, your ability and your worth?

If you have been able to answer that question, you will have picked out an area of symbiosis in your relationship.

There are, of course, areas in all relationships not affected by symbiosis: areas where both partners are free to grow and change without upsetting or interfering with the other's vested interests.

The areas free of symbiosis will not be disturbed if the relationship tie is broken, but the symbiotic parts will be severely disabled, at least for a while.

The effect of loss on symbiotic relationships

I discovered the effect of loss on symbiotic relationships after my mother died. I was still single at that point, and had little idea how dependent I was on her for my feelings of self-worth. All my life till then, I had had her there, believing in me. I had taken it for granted that she would do this for me. Suddenly, I could no longer take for granted that, whatever happened, someone would go on believing in my worth! I had other loving relatives, and many close friends, but somehow it felt as if, when Mum died, she had taken away with her all the feelings of self-esteem I had subconsciously invested in her safe-keeping.

My mother and father had shared the tasks of living together between them. Mum had taken care of the cooking, the laundry, the housework and most of the shopping, while Dad looked after the bills, the garden, and the car. We used to tease Dad that his cooking ability was limited to boiling an egg. But in his mid-seventies, he set about learning to cook what he wanted to eat. He did not choose to learn to bake, but his children soon knew that he appreciated it if they filled the freezer with baking when they visited! Inevitably, some things Mum had done for him were, from the time of her death, left undone. He lived without these.

Saul, King of Israel, had been dependent on the prophet Samuel for telling him the word of God in each new crisis during his reign. Samuel died, and Saul's enemies, the Philistines, came to attack him. Saul tried to find the word of God for himself, but no word came to tell him how to cope with this critical situation. In sheer desperation, Saul resorted to a line of action he had forbidden to others.

Turn to 1 Samuel 28 and read from verse 3 to discover how Saul attempted to fill the void left by Samuel's death.

The Adaptive Phase of Grief

Spiegel's final stage of the grief process (see p. 37) is the stage of adaptation—the stage of adapting to living without the person or thing you have lost. This can begin from the time the loss is acknowledged. It may even begin to happen before the loss actually occurs, if it is known about in advance. It cannot be completed until after the pain of the regressive phase has been lived through.

When you lose a person who has fulfilled your needs, you have to make new decisions about how you will adapt, in order to have these needs met. You have five options:

a) you can begin to meet your own needs
b) you can find others to meet your needs for you (including God)
c) you can decide to live with unmet needs
d) you can decide that you no longer need what once you did
e) you can pretend your needs no longer exist.

If you think about this in terms of investment, you can describe the grief process as one in which you gradually begin to withdraw from the lost relationship (job/ home/etc.) whatever you had invested in it. Once you withdraw it, you can keep it, or you can begin to re-invest it in other relationships, or in making life meaningful without paid employment, by making another house feel like home—in fact by doing whatever you need to do to make a new life for yourself.*

Trial Re-investments

If you have suffered a major loss, your investment in it will have been huge. In the period of adjustment before you re-invest a great deal into one relationship—for instance, before re-marriage—there might be a time when people try out various other people and interests, investing a small amount of time and energy and symbiotic need in each on a trial basis.

Often the more obvious needs, like the need for company, the need to talk over family responsibilities, the need for physical closeness, the need for help in very practical areas, are the ones which will get early attention. Later on a person will, usually unconsciously, try to have others meet the psychological symbiotic needs.

In this process of gradual readjustment, there seems to be a great need for people who are willing to give temporary help of various kinds and who will not feel let down if the same help is not asked for, again and again, in the context of a more

*You may wish to look back to the end of Chapter Three, where you thought about your adjustment to a personal loss.

permanent, growing relationship.

For instance, some people find great relief in talking to a total stranger—someone in the bus or in a launderette—someone who is willing to listen, and not to judge nor offer solutions. Others will take a small problem to the Citizen's Advice Bureau or the doctor—to someone whose job it is to give attention to the problem, but who will make no demands in return.

Carers, beware!

In the regressive phase of grief there can be such a need for someone to understand, that any prepared to listen may be told 'I don't know what I would do without you. I'm able to tell you things I've never told another living soul.' That can be immensely flattering for the understanding person!

The reality of the situation is that the grieving person will grow through that stage and no longer feel the need of the person who has been so crucial in the supporting role. The supporter, on the other hand, may have given hours of time to that relationship, at great personal cost, and may be expecting that a more permanent relationship would come out of it. Helpers have to expect to be 'grown out of', when the mourner is re-entering meaningful life again.

A number of people, professional and otherwise, find themselves in trouble because of this very factor.

One young minister became emotionally involved with an attractive young widow in his congregation. Her husband had died very tragically, and he had done his best to comfort and help her through a traumatic time. As the weeks went by, he became sexually involved with her. In spite of enormous guilt feelings about this, he felt he could not get out of the situation without damaging the widow, who had already suffered so much. He could not bring himself to go to anyone for help, nor could he think clearly about the situation. Months went by, while every other area of his life and work suffered.

Holiday time came. He went off with his wife and family.

Before they arrived back, the widow had left to visit relatives in Canada. With mixed emotions, he called to see her on her return. She was happy and excited, and wearing a new engagement ring. She had met an old school friend on her journey, and asked the minister if he would perform the wedding ceremony for them. Over and over again she thanked him, claiming that it was because of his relationship with her that she was now able to think of marrying again.

It took him at least a year of painful readjustment to recover from this rejection, to face up to his internal guilt, and to begin to feel ready to grow closer to his wife again.

New life, with new resources for helping others

It is a natural and healthy thing for a person to grow through loss and to come out the other end to make a new life.

Life does not go back to what it was before grief entered. Any person who has worked through a major grief situation will have discovered strengths and inner resources previously untapped. Many go into groups or organisations where they can be of some support to others, using their new insights and understanding.

Four crucial Questions

If growing through loss changes a person's life, it follows that he or she, whether consciously or not, will have to find new answers to certain basic questions. The questions will not be new. They are the ones each had to work on in childhood, and those which recur at every new stage on life's journey. They are very relevant as a mourner emerges from the grief process.

The questions are these:

1. Who am I?
    ... or who am I now, without X?

2. Who are all these other people?
   (What can I do for them, and what will they do for me?)
3. What am I doing here?
4. What happens to someone like me?

An Exercise

For you to think through, then to share with others

1. *If you have been working through an experience of loss, have a look at the four questions above.*
   a) *Before your loss, how might you have answered these?*
   b) *Since your recovery, how have your answers changed?*
2. *If you are helping others to work through an experience of loss, how might you use these four questions with them?*
3. *Jesus said 'Love your neighbour as yourself.' In your caring for people in grief, are you remembering to care also for yourself?*

. . . in the tender compassion of our God,
the morning sun from heaven will rise upon us,
to shine on those who live in darkness,
under the cloud of death,
and to guide our feet into the way of peace.

Luke 1 : 78–79. (N E B)